Value Driven
Enterprise Architecture

Cay Hasselmann

DEDICATION

To Jutta Hasselmann
for 17 wonderful years of marriage

CONTENTS

Foreword

If writers were good businessmen, they'd have too much sense to be writers.

Irvin S. Cobb

I started well over 2 years ago on a podcast covering Enterprise Architecture (The Critical Enterprise Architecture Netcast) as my wife suggested that I had a good voice and I was always passionate in sharing knowledge.

The podcast in turn led me to consider Enterprise Architecture much more in detail after producing the first 30 episodes, as they were just a rehash of the training that I gave architects in my various roles as a contractor and which were usually welcomed.

The first thing was that I really asked myself about the definition of Enterprise Architecture. That task in itself turned out to be complicated. I looked at various frameworks and discovered that enterprise architecture despite being described in great detail is still in the very early phases of its existence. So instead of defining enterprise architecture I started to explain all of the IT functions and the role of the Enterprise Architect within to ensure that Enterprise Architecture is not just created as a new island. In short CIO, Portfolio Manager and Enterprise Architect are the generalists in IT, with Enterprise Architect as the technical expert. Everyone else in IT takes a specialised place. The main responsibility of the Enterprise Architect is keeping the enterprise sound from a technical & process point, while the others look more on the management, the budget, business change management and the stakeholder management. All together are responsible for strategy.

Additionally I perceived that most of the Enterprise Architects were leaning towards Hubris (me included) and so often displayed a "God complex" in the dislike for following others work, with the exception of just seeing it as a good start with themselves refining it. This in term I have then seen in the production of many frameworks and an even higher number of papers on frameworks.

The three things that I found missing were simple concepts, a critical self reflection and a clear business case for Enterprise Architecture. So I started the second phase of the podcast in following these guidelines, even if I have not always stuck to this. So far the podcast has grown to the most popular in terms of subscribers in the architecture area.

I have received lots of good feedback in the last 2 years, but also a lot of critic response mainly in two areas. The first one comes down to the voice quality (I have no recording studio and many podcasts are produced after a long work day) and on my German accent (which I have problems hiding). The second area is also an area were I get praise on the other hand. The complaints were mainly in the area that I am not academic, too pragmatic, too commercial, too managerial, too delivery focused and I am not building on the established frameworks.

After deciding to write this book I decided to write a book based on the commercial, pragmatic, not academic and delivery focused area of Enterprise Architecture without building on existing frameworks, which I in general find very valuable. So with this book I want to try to establish a different starting point for Enterprise Architecture.

So if you will disagree with the concept, but can find some value in the concepts or just in the reference material I am more than happy to have invested some time.

As in the podcasts please send any comments to cay@accent.li

Cay Hasselmann

1. Introduction

You don't want another Enron? Here's your law: If a company, can't explain, in ONE SENTENCE....what it does....it's illegal.

Lewis Black

I am creating this book as an introduction into the Value Driven Enterprise Architecture not to point out flaws in other frameworks or to even build on an existence work. My goal is not to discredit any other methodologies; however I will make references to other Enterprise Architecture methodologies and describe why I find them beneficial or where I have problems in following them.

The Value Driven Enterprise Architecture should only be used if the enterprise is primary motivated by profit and/or by GRC (Governance, Risk & Compliance) Management, as pointed out in chapter 2.

Enterprise Architecture is about creating value in IS (or IT). The value consists of three factors:

- ✓ Reduction of the overall total cost of ownership
- ✓ Reduction of the overall risks
- ✓ A faster time to market of IS Services

Anything that is not geared towards these values should not be done. So Enterprise Architecture is not:

- Creating frameworks for the reason of having frameworks
- Creating strategies that are based on principles other than the 3 goals

- Documenting and discovering any "wrong doing" and calling it governance

- Coming up with a too neat and clean solution as IS is dirty

- Creating theoretical frameworks

- Implementing Enterprise Architecture artefact's without any tangible benefits

- Creating an Enterprise Architecture function

- Creating a science to justify higher salaries

If we take the 3 values into closer considerations there are only a few tasks that Enterprise Architecture can deliver for all of these values:

- Practical reuse of the existing IS assets

- Process execution and improvement of the IS processes

- Use of standard business processes

There are also three more areas that would satisfy all the goals:

- Formulate an effective strategy and prioritise

- Risk reward, net present value and business change management

- Service Operation, Transition and Contentious Performance Improvement Management

These areas are usually covered by the CIO, portfolio and service management. In those areas the enterprise architect may be a major contributor or not, see chapter 4.

This statement is in violation with several enterprise architects and some frameworks; however in the value driven enterprise architecture I am focusing more on the doable and less on the academic side.

This list that mainly only consists of three tasks represent almost the entirety of the value driven Enterprise Architecture. This may be a shock for many Enterprise Architects as it reduces the complexity to a point that everyone can understand it.

The skill of the value driven Enterprise Architecture is in the merits of profession, NOT in way that everything is complicated. At the end through all business activity it always comes down to the fact that if it is complex it is not going to last, but if everything is build on simple steps it usually succeeds.

There are some other tasks that deliver two or only one of these values, however since they are of less value impact their description has to wait for some later point, as we all will first start to implement the tasks that have the largest return of investment.

In the following chapters I will first explain the detailed tasks are behind the three tasks. Once I have documented this I will then try to explain the process to execute the tasks and in the final part I will create a knowledge base or a reference for the before mentioned skills. As always I will try to keep it as generic as possible rather than to go in great detail and get lost.

Within all chapters I will only skim the surface as to document all processes, all business architecture and all the standard services that can be considered as standards will not fit in this book. So I will hopefully continue with further reference books on all these subjects under the condition that this book will at least pay for itself in this very niche market.

2. Motivation for enterprise architecture

Never let an inventor run a company. You can never get him to stop tinkering and bring something to market.

E. F. Schumacher

There are 5 general approaches in enterprise architecture at any organisation.

For enterprise architecture it is important to understand that it is only possible to follow one approach, while then using a secondary approach for verification if it is not possible to decide a priority on the first one.

There are many enterprise architects that try to make it right for everyone in same way as this happens in other areas. So it is important to determine the main motivations of the enterprise even if they are contrary to a given framework.

Enterprise Architecture always needs to be serving the enterprise not the other way around. I am sure that some Enterprise Architects will not see it that way; however I cannot see that Enterprise Architecture will dictate the company strategies and business plans. So for my part Enterprise Architecture is part of IT and not some super important function that is par with the CIO.

To understand the enterprise it is important to understand the 5 most used motivation options with a small SWOT analysis on each option.

2.1. Option 1: Financial value approach

Option 1 concentrates on enterprises that are mainly motivated by profits. Not all commercial entities are however mainly motivated by money as some follow more traditional lines. This approach often used by Controllers and Operational Executives, as well as the most prevalent one as most enterprises are focused on profits.

The main enterprise architecture tasks in this option are:

- Sort the IS Services in high, medium, low and none value

- Phase out IS Services with no value, retain and not invest new in those of low value, expand on the high value ones and then of those with medium value

- Create a 3 different virtual IS environment based on the value and invest accordingly.

- Create IS value portfolio enterprise architecture

SWOT

- Strength: IS is business value driven, easy prioritisation, creates highest value of IS

- Weaknesses: Requires transformation on how IS is operating, hard to push through special projects

- Opportunities: Creates an even playing field for all areas of the business, usually easy to create quick wins

- Threads: Usually likely to create many specialised Services instead of a fully integrated system

8

2.2. Option 2: Principle based approach

Some public bodies are based on principles rather than profits, you also find this approach in some non for profit enterprises that are usually following a set of ethics. This approach is often used by IS Architects and Managers, however it should be noted that it is only successful if the rest of the enterprise can follow the same option.

The main enterprise architecture tasks in this option are:

- Handle all IS Services equally with the exception of the Service Levels

- Prioritise work based on general Business and IT principles

- Establish technical and business architecture standards to control cost

- Establish a principle based enterprise architecture

SWOT

- Strength: Easy to understand, easy to adopt

- Weaknesses: Will create long debates on each work, usually will delay decisions

- Opportunities: High acceptance with good cultural acceptance

- Threads: Creates enterprises with unclear structures

2.3 Option 3: Strategic value approach

Some enterprises are driven by strategy to the extend that this is the main driver. The problematic area is just that the strategy is only sometimes used, as it is virtually impossible to get any hard numbers and is often not very detailed. The only enterprises that are really following a strategic value approach companies with a solid profit or public organisations that are lead by a charismatic CEO.

The main enterprise architecture tasks in this option are:

- All IS Services are solely group according to the strategic value indicator

- Only those IS Services that are associated with a high strategic value will be expanded, all other Services (e.g. usually administration and support processes) will only be retained

- Establish a strategic driven enterprise architecture

SWOT

- Strength: Concentrates IS Services on main challenges

- Weaknesses: Usually supporting processes will always be de-prioritised

- Opportunities: Easy way to drive change through an organisation

- Threads: Often fosters large IS projects with missing cost controls and no real business value

2.4 Option 4: Business requirements approach

The business requirements approach is the most used traditional approach and is used if there is no clear IS leadership in an enterprise. Approach often used by heads of departments as it is a nice way to rule parts of the enterprise as fiefdoms as it is easy to state requirements without any case and it makes heads the most important rulers as they formulate the requirements in their stove-pipes or islands.

The main enterprise architecture tasks in this option are:

- Traditional approach to priorities all IS Services based on a business requirements usually through a budget rounds driven approach

- IS Services will be closely linked to a business project

- Standardisation of IS Services to help to create common Services to drive down costs

- Establish a supporting enterprise architecture to help keep commonality

SWOT

- Strength: Easy acceptance, business budget driven

- Weaknesses: Usually best connected faction will reach most, often creates scope creep

- Opportunities: Easy to follow process

- Threads: Less stability because of constant requirement change, fragmentation of IS.

2.5 Option 5: GRC approach I

This approach based on governance, risk and compliance management is used in all industries that have experienced some mayor crisis, are heavily regulated (e.g. Banks or Insurance) or are public bodies. Virtually always there are some sets of special regulations (e.g. Basel III or Solvency II) in place. Usually this approach is used by legal, risk management, compliance and security officers

The main enterprise architecture tasks in this option are:

- Enterprise Architecture will ensure that IS Services are geared towards the smallest risk basis with a maximum of compliance against the regulations.

- Enterprise architecture will enable a strong governance function to move all IS Services towards a high capability maturity level (CMMI)

SWOT

- Strength: Creates mature and well designed IS Services that stand up against external scrutiny

- Weaknesses: Usually lengthens time to market

- Opportunities: Helps IS to mature as a valuable function

- Threads: Creates a restricted or bureaucratic environment with a lack of original initiative

Once the motivation option is understood it is important to fine tune the Enterprise Architecture accordingly. For example it will only make sense that you use the TOGAF ADM if the Enterprise follows option 4 as main motivation with option 2 in second place.

Often forgetting on these motivations is the reason that some successes in one enterprise are hard to replicate in another.

The ways of executing enterprise architecture as discussed in this book follows option 1 and 5 and it should be noted that it is not advisable to use the Value Driven Enterprise Architecture for enterprises that are scoring high on option 2, 3 and 4.

3. Practical reuse of the existing IS assets

Informed decision-making comes from a long tradition of guessing and then blaming others for inadequate results.

Scott Adams

3.1. Value

If we reuse existing assets we should be able to save costs by not investing to much new money (there are always costs reoccurring in the IS department, mine as an Enterprise Architect for example). The specific way that we are describing the enterprise architecture here via a service catalogue will also enable us to prioritise all IS Services in term of their business value, thereby identifying all Services with a negative net present value, at the same time we will also enable the IS function to charge back the Services offered and as such being able to truly calculate any cost to the business.

The risks are lowered if we reuse existing proven assets (this of course always comes with the caveat that the existing assets are proven :-)

The faster time to market stems from the fact that no new mayor design, architecture, development and/or build, test, deployment, transition, operational readiness, supplier management, etc.. is needed (again this builds on the assumption that the current IS assets are proven)

3.2. Introduction

To reuse IS assets it is first important to understand the existing IS assets. As an asset register for IS assets it is best to use a simple IS Service Catalogue that will list all IS Services from the power service towards IS Business Services such as a Document management service and interrelate them against each other. This IS asset register should state

- Service description

- Unit of service (e.g. 1GB on a SAN)

- Any service level agreement that is associated with the service

- Any service level requirement that is associated with an IS Business Service,

- The Service owner

- The Service design authority

- The associated costs based on a 5 year TCO on the unit

- The service supplier

- A technical description

- Any legacy dependencies

This exercise should take about 2-3 month for an average sized enterprise to get it up to 80 % complete based on the constraint that if there is no SLA or SLR the fact is just to be noted. To create this register or catalogue I will describe the L6 +1 process later. The service catalogue should also be as neutral as possible describing a small server, rather than the specification of the server as this will change too fast. It is also important not to spend more than a couple of days in creating the database and GUI for this register, as the content is far more important than the display. If you mail me I am able to provide a database or just the ERD at no cost.

Once the service catalogue is in place there are some instant benefits against the values:

- ➤ Identification of multiple applications performing the same service --) cost reduction in merging same functionality

- ➤ Any new project can instantly gather the TCO from this catalogue and explore the reusable parts (this will usually reduce the costs of a project by 10 % and 20 on time)

- ➤ Design and architecture will be able to reference clear objects

- ➤ Reduced time for service transition and testing as the Services are already in place

- ➤ Reduced risks in reusing clearly described and proven Services

The next step is than to maintain this register and prioritise the IS assets in the IS strategy to drive further benefits, as well as to improve the SLA, SLR and the other surrounding dependencies on each service.

Once the IS asset register or catalogue is in place it is important to link the IS Business Services to the existing business processes (if they are known and documented).

The processes themselves need to be linked to the KPI's of the enterprise and to the products or Services offered by the company.

All the products or Services than need to be linked to their financial value in terms of their profitability; in the same way the business processes will need to be evaluated by against their legal, risk and compliant value.

This way it is possible to measure all the business processes and the associated IS Services to their businesses value. The business value will also enable to objectively prioritise (not dependant on the business owner who also will tell you that his/her service is the most important one) and to calculate the Net Present Value (NPV) of the IS Services. Should the NPV be negative and the legal, risk and compliant value also low (in my experience usually true for 20 % of all Services) a plan for their retirement should be drafted to save costs on the missing value preposition.

Finally the information gathered will also enable the IS department to cross charge for all the IS Services. These cross charging will usually also help to retire the service of negative business value from the organisation.

For the reuse of Services itself the service will require to be compatible with each other, which is not usually the case so an interaction of the various Services will need to be set up on an open standard.

It is very important at this juncture that the enterprise architect will have to insist reusing existing Services even if they are less than ideal and only invest into new Services if they are non existent. Usually at this point there is a tendency to spend a lot of money in redefining Services for common usage. However this in itself usually destroys the value based positive net present value of the value driven enterprise architecture in itself. It should also be noted that the enterprise architect should mainly define the services, the service strategy and the standards, while leaving the details of the architecture to other architects.

The full impact of benefits of the IS asset register is when it is used in conjunction with a standard IS business process as described in chapter 4.

3.3. The detailed enterprise architecture process

The detailed process will cover the IT asset register, the strategic impact and the financials.

3.3.1. Creation of a service catalogue

The creation of the service catalogue is a team effort where the Enterprise Architect need to involve all parties, so it is essential that all information is gathered in a simple not to misunderstandable way. I will not actual provide a service catalogue tool here, but I am happy to send any reader a link with the database containing the catalogue.

Usually it is best to start with the IS Services before defining the IS Business Services, some may even argue that you can only define an IS Business Services with a given requirement, but that is rather arguing if chicken or egg came first. For this task a retro perspective approach will be allowed.

An IS-Service always consists of a description, a Service Design Authority, cost and a SLA.

When starting to define IS-Services the two most important things are to create the description and the rudimentary SLA, as the SLA may split what you think of one IS-Service into many. Even owner and information can be entered in a second iteration.

An IS-Service usually is linked to many other IS Services. To ensure that you are now not starting to create a very complex picture it is advisable to follow some best practises like the L6 Model (I made up the name myself) here.

The L6 Model

The L6 model consists of 6 levels with Level 1 as the IS Services nearest to the Business Services and Level 6 the furthest apart. In the following I will describe the model with some examples:

Level 1   Application related IS Services   e.g. ERP A, Legacy Apps, CRM B

Level 2   Supporting IS Services   e.g. Adobe Forms, SharePoint Services

Level 3   Technical IS Services   e.g. AD, DB's, DNS, LDAP

Level 4   OS & Virtualisation IS Services   e.g. Linux, Windows, Hyper V

Level 5   Hardware IS Services   e.g. Servers, Switches, SAN

Level 6   Infrastructure IS Services   e.g. cabinets, power, cabling

All trademarks or registered trademarks are the property of their respective owners.

Now it is important that you work the model from L6 upwards and always remember to specify the Services with the SLA, so it is not unlikely that e.g. you end up with 10 IS-Services that are all called Windows OS but carry different SLA's (due to security, availability, etc...). Once you reach Level 1 it is very easy to chose all the associated more technical Services against the application. If you try it the other way you will almost always fail or spend 15 times as long, which is what all the strategic thinkers usually do ;-)

Tools such as used for development or testing are best put in level 2.

For level 1 and 2 it is best first to list all the tool and applications and then later create a service. An example for this could be an open source development service that will consist of 20 tools and applications that make the service. On the other hand it is also possible that a single ERP system can result in very many application Services.

Additional a measurement should be attached in describing a unit with the associated costs. This is usually done by adding all the costs for implementation and running the service for 5 years into one lump sum and then dividing it according to the unit size.

So let us start with an example for a storage service based on a SAN in Level 5. The assumption is that we have already defined the Level 6 Services as follows (simplified):

ID	IS_SLA	SDA	Service_Supplier	Unit_Description
1	No SLA in place	Hans Seul	Corporate Services	Office Power
2	24*7	Paul Smith	Corporate Services	3 Tier server room power
3	24*7	Paul Smith	Corporate Services	Server room cooling
4	No SLA in place	Paul Smith	Corporate Services	Office cooling
5	24*7	Paul Smith	Corporate Services	Server room protection services
6	No SLA in place	Paul Smith	Corporate Services	Com. room protection services
7	No SLA in place	Paul Smith	Corporate Services	Office protection services

Now for the SAN service we first define that this is a SAN with a SLA as follows:

- ✓ Security – non standard encryption, dedicated VLAN, own security segment

- ✓ Capacity – 460 TB (effective storage)

- ✓ Availability – 24 *5 in GMT

- ✓ Uptime 99.9 %

- ✓ Continuity Required to be near real mirror to disaster recovery site

- ✓ Reaction time 2.3 ms average I/O with no more than 5 ms maximum.

- ✓ Problem Response Time : see Operational Service Agreement A2

- ✓ Incident Response Time : see Operational Service Agreement A2

- ✓ Business Value: No Value yet

The Service Supplier will be the In-house Service Management and the Service Design Authority will be Ben Barber.

Now there are two more tasks left. First there will be the associations with the Level 6 Services such as Number 3, 4 and 6.

Second there is the need to calculate the costs. For cost calculations the TCO (as an example) is calculated as below:

✓ Implementation costs	40,000 $
✓ Hardware costs	400,000 $
✓ Licence costs	25,000 $
✓ 5 year maintenance costs (5 % p.a.)	6,250 $
✓ Support costs (7 man days per month with 600 $ per man day)	252,000 $

(7 * 12 Month * 5 years * 600 $)

So the TCO for 5 years is 723,250 $ or 1.54 $ per GB. So if now in any project a project manager will do his calculation he/she will just use the given GB from an architect and multiply them with 1.54. Additional he/she will then do the same for the associated Services.

So after doing the work for Level 6 to 3 the catalogue for an average organisation could look something like this:

ID	IS_SLA	Service_Cost per_Unit	Unit_Description
1	No SLA in place		Office Power
2	24*7		3 Tier server room power
3	24*7		Server room cooling
4	No SLA in place		Office cooling
5	24*7		Server room protection services
6	No SLA in place		Com. room protection services
7	No SLA in place		Office protection services
8	No SLA in place	£3,000.00	Server room cabinets 16 inch
9	No SLA in place	£3,000.00	Com. room cabinets 16 inch
10	24*7		Network cabling (inc. patching panel)
11	No SLA in place		KVM cabling
12	24*7		Connection to external parties
13	No SLA in place		Offsite storage
14	24*7		Server room switches
15	No SLA in place		Office switches
16	No SLA in place		Router
17	No SLA in place		Firewalls
18	No SLA in place	£12.14	SAN cost per GB
19	No SLA in place	£2.20	New DAS per GB
20	No SLA in place	£1.10	Old DAS per GB
21	24*7	£34,375.00	Small 24*7 server
22	No SLA in place	£4,875.00	Small 10*5 server
23	24*7	£42,500.00	Medium 24*7 server
24	No SLA in place	£13,000.00	Medium 10*5 server
25	24*7	£61,250.00	Large 24*7 server
26	No SLA in place	£31,750.00	Large 10*5 server
27	No SLA in place	£2.53	Multifunctional printer per 1000 pages
28	No SLA in place		Colour Printer
29	No SLA in place		B/W Printer
30	No SLA in place	£10,000.00	Plotter
32	No SLA in place		Tape library
34	No SLA in place	£500.00	Normal performance desktop
35	No SLA in place	£1,875.00	High performance desktop
36	No SLA in place	£750.00	Normal performance laptop
37	No SLA in place	£2,500.00	High performance laptop
38	No SLA in place	£6.00	Normal mobile phone
39	No SLA in place	£100.00	Smartphone
40	No SLA in place	£250.00	Normal desk phone

41	No SLA in place	£400.00	Director's desk phone
42	No SLA in place	£400.00	Extended desk phone
43	No SLA in place	£150.00	Standard display
44	No SLA in place	£20.00	Standard HID
45	No SLA in place	£2,500.00	IP conferencing system
46	No SLA in place	£20,000.00	PBX conferencing system
47	No SLA in place	£1,000.00	Beamer
48	24*7	£40,000.00	Windows 2003 Clustered
49	No SLA in place	£31,500.00	Windows 2003 DMZ
50	No SLA in place	£31,500.00	Windows 2003 LAN
51	No SLA in place	£31,500.00	Windows 2008 DMZ
52	No SLA in place	£31,500.00	Windows 2008 LAN
53	No SLA in place	£250.00	Windows XP imaged
54	No SLA in place	£500.00	Windows XP non imaged
55	No SLA in place	£250.00	Windows 7 imaged
56	No SLA in place	£500.00	Windows 7 non imaged
57	No SLA in place	£31,500.00	Red Hat
58	No SLA in place	£33,500.00	VM Ware normal
59	24*7	£49,000.00	VM Ware high available
60	No SLA in place	£1,000.00	Upgrade device OS
61	24*7	£95,000.00	Symantec cluster service
62	24*7	£37,500.00	MS cluster Service
63	24*7	£70,000.00	HA cluster (VMWare)
67	No SLA in place	£66,500.00	Normal Oracle DB
68	24*7	£83,000.00	HA Oracle DB
69	No SLA in place	£33,500.00	MS SQL DB
70	24*7	£35,000.00	HA MS SQL DB
71	24*7	£16,500.00	HA My SQL DB
72	No SLA in place	£1,000.00	Upscale MS Access
73	No SLA in place	£250.00	MS Access
74	No SLA in place		Internal AD & DNS
75	No SLA in place		External AD & DNS
76	No SLA in place		DHCP
77	No SLA in place		SEP
78	24*7		VPN
79	No SLA in place	£100.00	Cryptographic Services
80	No SLA in place		Polar auditor
81	No SLA in place		CA service
82	No SLA in place		Protection Manager
83	No SLA in place		Proxy Service

At this stage it is important to point out that one should not focus on a specific specification for a service, but rather quote a small, medium and large server with the current specification. With OS and other software products often a pragmatic view on license needs to be taken as they are sold in volume licensing and as such are hard to calculate on a single copy; however usually the support costs are the bulk of the 5 year TCO.

When moving to Level 2 it is first important to determine all the tools around the enterprise. Once this done the Enterprise Architect can then make sense of how best to sort them for example in reporting tool Services, development environment Services and so on. Here one of the biggest challenges is to extract the SLA, as developers and software architects always want to have Service Level Requirements for SLA or Non Functional Requirements from others, but are seldom happy of defining their own ones for their Services.

Level 1 and IS Business Services are properly the hardest, but also the most fun once to document for Enterprise Architects.

Here it is first important to get a list of all applications without thinking of Services in the first place.

After this is done all applications need to be described with a single summary phrase. Once this is done an interesting thing is happening. Often there are 5 to 15 applications that get the same phrase. This phrase is what we will call IS Business Services. As an example usually there are often some applications that are a Business Case Management service (or applications). For this service there are now some IS application services. In the given example of the IS business service of the Business Case Management service they could be:

- ✓ Work flow Service (one work flow)

- ✓ Rule Service (one Business Rule)

- ✓ Documentation Management Service (one Doc. Type)

- ✓ Authentication Service (I user group)

- ✓ Recording Service (1 GUI)

- ✓ Reporting Service (1 average report)

- ✓ Meta Data Reference Service (1 Table)

- ✓ Resource Management Service (1 resource or asset type)

- ✓ Resource Management Service (1 resource or asset type)

- ✓ Analytic Service (1 report)

- ✓ Integration Service (1 average interface)

- ✓ Quality Service(based on Application X)

Please note that each Application service will always need a unit associated so that we can price them.

If we now take another IS Business service such as a Compensation service that will ensure that someone is compensated for work done; the IS Application Services associated will be:

- ✓ Recording Service (1 GUI)

- ✓ Work flow Service (one work flow)

- ✓ Integration Service (1 average interface)

- ✓ Documentation Management Service (one Document Type)

- ✓ Reporting Service (1 average report)

- ✓ Rule Service (one Business Rule)

Here are already two different IS business services that have some similar IS application services that they share.

Before we now concentrate on the IS application services we first need to spend some time on the IS business services. The first task is to find an owner for the service, which is usually harder said than done, as the service is used by many different parts of the business. Once an owner is found the Service requires a Service Level Requirement to determine the SLA for the associated IS application service.

After this we are looking again at the IS application services. We know the required SLA for each of them and can determine the TCO for each one and all the associated Services as well. At this junction it is often important to alert the IS Business service Owner on the TCO for his/her service, which will usually lead to a lesser SLR. However with a lesser SLR you also usually have higher risks that the owner will need to sign and the risk matrix needs to be stored with the service. This way a good balance on cost versus risks can be reached.

Now is also the time to describe if the existing IS application services are reusable for the future. At that point any Enterprise Architect will need to classify at least half of the services as reusable; as there is a dynamic on architects in general always to create new services as reusable and then call the whole exercise reusing, even if it is not. So any value based approach will need to invest very good thinking and a skill for compromise to show the reusability at this point.

Once this is accomplished most Services will still not have any business value associated with them. This exercise often also known by project managers as prioritising is a very hard one if it is not done with a methodology.

To accomplish this, the IS business services will now need to be associated with the Business Processes of your enterprise. The Business Processes are defined in most enterprises as most enterprises have signed up for ISO 9001 certification. Sometimes some Business Processes will need to be re-defined as they are only described in very elementary format. If that is the case chapter 5 of this book might help.

Once all IS business services are lined up with the Business Processes there is the need to associate all Business Processes with the Business Products and services of the enterprise.

26

The Products and Services of the enterprise then need to be sorted in terms of their financial impact by the financial controllers in terms of 1 to 10 (never ask them for the real numbers as they are sensitive business information).

With this information a financial value can then be attempted. Once all business processes have been scored it is important to check the results back with the financial Controllers. After this it is also important to have the chief legal counsel and the head of risk score all the Business Processes from 1 to 10. At the end it might also be good to have the Business Processes owner score them as well, however they will almost ever give a high score for their own processes. So at the end if you combine all the scores you will have the real value of all the Business Processes and their associated IS business services and the IS services. If you however only rely on the Business Process Owners the score will be very inconclusive.

3.3.2. Define strategic assets

Within the service catalogue there are now some potential redundant services, as it is usually the case in any organisation that the same service was produced with different tools.

Before defining services as strategic assets it is important to look at the IS strategy as a process rather than as jolly nice endeavour in more detail. The IS processes in general will be part of chapter 4, however the strategy process as drafted in appendix A will be discussed in part here. In this chapter only the first Level 2 processes in strategy are required and discussed.

So before starting with the strategy on defining the Services there is a need to look at the market definition as we should not drop in the same old way as in the early stages of enterprise architecture, where everything was based on some theoretical lines based on the ideal world and how things should be done, rather how the market looks for the enterprise we are in. This process is then described in detail on 4 level 3 processes. Once we understand the strategic market forces we will then look at the actual strategic defining of the Services, where our service catalogue will show up again.

On all the strategic processes please note that the processes are always performed by a mix of the CIO, the portfolio managers and the enterprise architects in a team rather by one role in isolation. I have therefore used many frameworks (detail in chapter 4) and some experience to combine the best practises rather then to stick to an ideal scenario where the enterprise architects will live on their own little island and critic everyone else on living on their islands.

At this point please excuse my missing graphical skills to keep all EPC's in ratio as it is hard enough to put a process on any paper that is less then DIN A2, so for all of you that have worked as a business analyst in the past this should be familiar.

3.3.2.1 Market definition strategy

Within the market definition strategy that is very similar to strategies in other departments than IS; each process will be shown as an EPC diagram with explanations given.

3.3.2.1.1 Competitive services strategy

The competitive service strategy is one of the longest single processes in IS strategy not only because it covers so many demanding task, but also because many of the tasks will require a substantial time commitment from the CIO. So there is the real risk that it never happens.

At this point it is obvious that there is the need of an additional project management to accomplish the process in itself. It is also usually wise to involve the corporate strategy team in this process. From my experience they will be very interested as they themselves usually are not working to any given process.

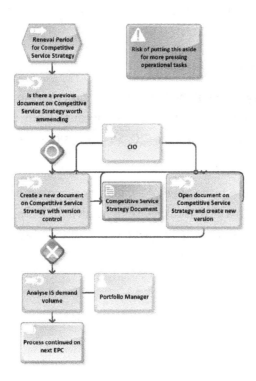

Renewal Period for Competitive Service Strategy

Risk of putting this aside for more pressing operational tasks

Is there a previous document on Competitive Service Strategy worth ammending

CIO

Create a new document on Competitive Service Strategy with version control

Competitive Service Strategy Document

Open document on Competitive Service Strategy and create new version

Analyse IS demand volume

Portfolio Manager

Process continued on next EPC

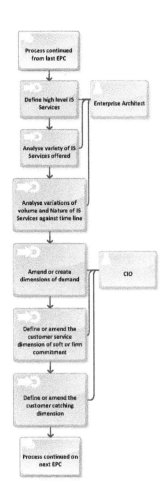

Process continued
from last EPC

Define high level IS
Services

Enterprise Architect

Analyse variety of IS
Services offered

Analyse variations of
volume and Nature of IS
Services against time line

Amend or create
dimensions of demand

CIO

Define or amend the
customer service
dimension of soft or firm
commitment

Define or amend the
customer catching
dimension

Process continued on
next EPC

31

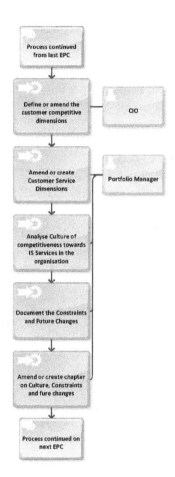

32

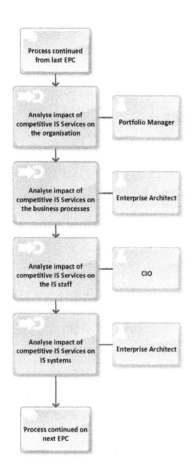

Process continued
from last EPC

Analyse impact of
competitive IS Services on
the organisation — Portfolio Manager

Analyse impact of
competitive IS Services on
the business processes — Enterprise Architect

Analyse impact of
competitive IS Services on
the IS staff — CIO

Analyse impact of
competitive IS Services on
IS systems — Enterprise Architect

Process continued on
next EPC

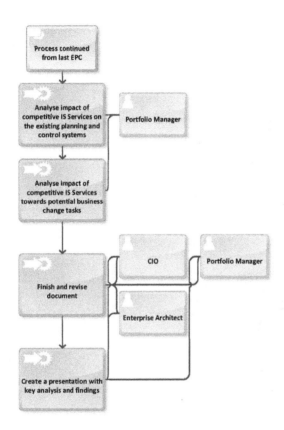

Process continued from last EPC

Analyse impact of competitive IS Services on the existing planning and control systems

Portfolio Manager

Analyse impact of competitive IS Services towards potential business change tasks

Finish and revise document

CIO

Portfolio Manager

Enterprise Architect

Create a presentation with key analysis and findings

One of the general observations that I have seen in helping implementing this process is that it takes many rounds of discussions to convince people to do any work of internal competitive analysis in IS.

To the best of my experience this process should be done every two years and because it requires so much work should be introduced in the budget as its own small project.

At the end of this exercise we now have a true picture on the enterprise drivers on competitive factors that will help the IS department to react on the value based structures of the market and also understand the internal competitive structure. It is not uncommon that after the results of this process the IT Department is restructured to allow for a better commercial positioning.

3.3.2.1.2 Understand customers

Understanding the customer is a more common strategic task that is executed quite common in many IS departments.

Understanding customers will always start with the definition of the term customers, as there are so many definitions it is always best that the CIO decides. Once the decision is done it is important to refer to all the existing strategy on understanding customers that the enterprise has already defined. This is normally contained in the marketing strategy. Only for those customers that cannot be found in these documents own work should be done.

Understanding the competitive side as well as the customers are the most important strategic input for nearly all decisions on an enterprise wide level and therefore it is highly advised not to skip these two processes.

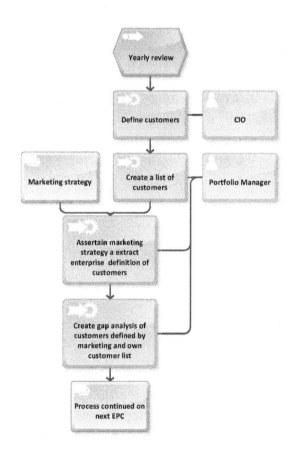

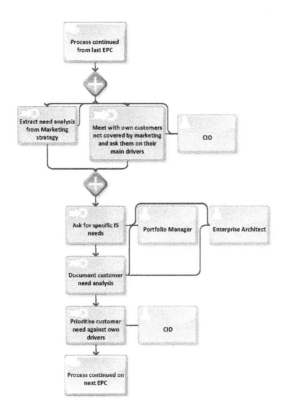

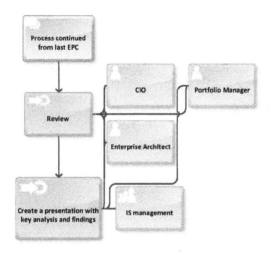

3.3.2.1.3 Identify opportunities

Many frameworks will try to assign the identification of priorities to one specific group only. This in itself is quite dangerous as there are opportunities in the various different areas of IS. Therefore I have created this process from 7 other "island" centric processes of various frameworks. The identification of increased throughput is best done by comparing some selected services from the service catalogue with that in other enterprises. It is normally quite easy to do that as other enterprises are also interested to see how well they are doing and only requires a standard NDA, so that any results are not to be used for embarrassing or spying but are just contained as a measurement for capabilities. The increased return on investment on the other hand is an area where the enterprise architect can explore the benefits of standardisation.

I should be noted that the 7th task in this process is equal with the fifth chapter of this book.

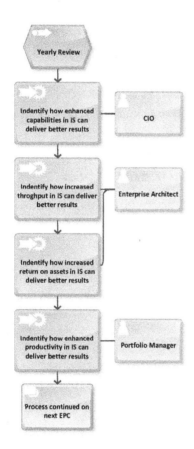

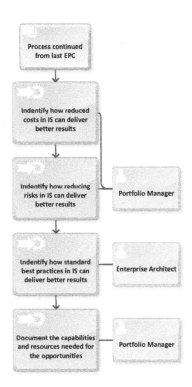

Process continued from last EPC

Indentify how reduced costs in IS can deliver better results

Indentify how reducing risks in IS can deliver better results — Portfolio Manager

Indentify how standard best practices in IS can deliver better results — Enterprise Architect

Document the capabilities and resources needed for the opportunities — Portfolio Manager

41

3.3.2.1.4 Classify opportunities

For opportunities to have any meaningful place in the IS life cycle the opportunities need to be classified.

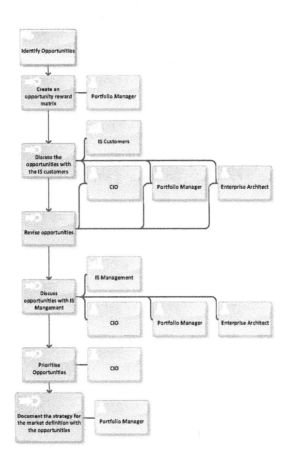

3.3.2.2 Define strategic assets

After finishing the strategic market definition this chapter is about really defining and dissecting the services that were discovered during the production of the service catalogue. It is just important to note that it is important not to skip the market definition as it is otherwise not possible to execute this process with its full benefits.

3.3.2.2.1 Define services

This process that is done solely by the enterprise architect is very simple if the market definition has been done and only focuses on defining any missing service.

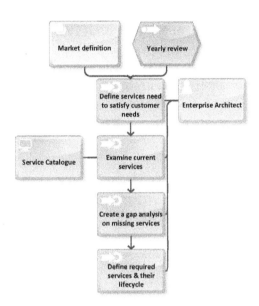

3.3.2.2.2 Define priorities

Within this processes the Services are ordered into priorities that we will then use in chapter 3.3.2.3 when we are executing on the strategy.

It should be noted that it is important that this process is done by the portfolio manager and not by the enterprise architect, to ensure that the strategy for the execution is not done by the same role in the enterprise that will oversee the execution thereof.

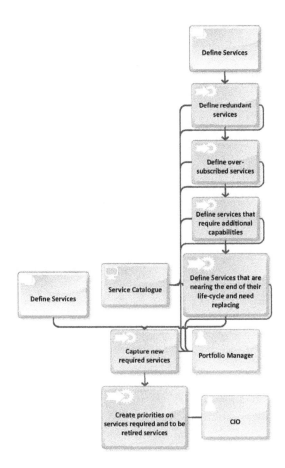

Define Services

Define redundant services

Define over-subscribed services

Define services that require additional capabilities

Define Services that are nearing the end of their life-cycle and need replacing

Define Services

Service Catalogue

Capture new required services

Portfolio Manager

Create priorities on services required and to be retired services

CIO

3.3.2.2.3 Define risk & compliance profile

The last level 3 process is important so that the risk and compliance factors are not lost as they often do if a value led approach is chosen.

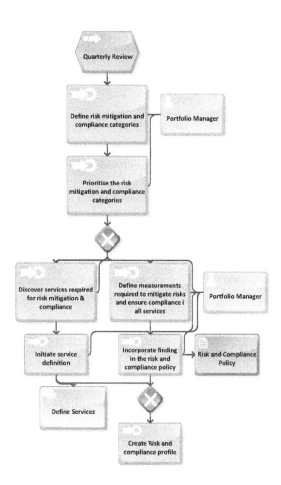

3.3.3. Execute strategy & eliminate multiple services

The first step is to execute the creation of new Services and the change to existing Services that will be discussed in chapter 4 of the book down to each task, as it requires a process driven architecture to ensure that the whole area of a service driven approach continues after its initial set-up. There are many good and even bad examples for this in many large enterprises. The value and service driven approach can only work in the long run if all people in the IS department of the enterprise are sticking to described processes, including the enterprise architects.

The next step is to look at the oversubscribed Services, as this is always an area for quick and easy wins. An example where a service is often oversubscribed is clusters for High Availability. In this area first make sure that the SLA's are at least similar.

Then explore the service to keep based on the value preposition on cost, risk and time to market. If you now have many different cluster services first identify the reason behind this. If you discover that certain applications will only work with a given number of cluster technologies then make a list for each and try to find a common platform. Once you still have a choice left look at the 5 year TCO as recorded in the service catalogue (and not the original flawed estimate from Project management), after this check on risks, however always remember that the services in IT have a maximum life cycle of 5 years, so arguments if the company is still there in 7 years are a non risk. Try only to focus on risks in the next year as with IT the technology is just too quick for longer considerations. At the end still remember if you have a solution for the service that has just a slightly higher cost, but enables a much quicker deployment you with consider this one.

Once you have chosen the one solution to stay, you will need to initiate a project with the business case we have produced in the strategic work and address this to the portfolio management. Once it is assigned as a project make sure that you and the portfolio manager are part of the steering group to ensure governing the project so that the value prepositions are kept in line, as there will certainly be some people who will try to build something new instead of just migrating all the eliminated solutions to the chosen solution.

An area that should not be attempted to clean up in retrospective are oversubscribed IS application Services that are customer facing, as any change seen by the user that was not initiated by him/her is always highly problematic. In that case just wait for the next mayor update. An example that I have often found in many enterprises is that of multiple different instances of a business case management application as an IS business service. Here it is advisable to gradually upgrade them all into the chosen standard service platform starting with invisible IS Services such as the business rule system and then only changing the Services with a GUI (such as the recording or reporting service) if an upgrade in capabilities is scheduled in the release management.

The last part of execution is to create a project brief for the redundant Services. Here it is important again that you as the enterprise architect with the portfolio manager will need to govern these projects very closely, as there is always lots of resistance in eliminating Services, as every service will always maintain the job of a few IT staff in the enterprise and they will start to come up with all kind of obstructions. Always remember it is relative simple to create a service that will put people in employment, but much harder to cut the cost and have redundancies.

3.4 Value check

When implementing the processes it is very important to always maintain an eye on the value, the risk reduction and the faster time to market.

3.4.1 Costs (ROI)

On costs or ROI this should be done in two stages. After the completion of the asset register it is important to follow up, how many Services are reused, how much time is saved on early stages on projects and how much effort is saved on Service management. The result is then likely to be used to build up enough momentum for the second phase.

In the second phase it is important to note down the less time spent in defining and designing the needs, the time saved in less failure due to a clear guidance (hard to record, therefore easier to estimate and sign off by the CIO), reduction of cost on Services made redundant or eliminated due to over-subscription .

The main problem that enterprise architects will be facing on the ROI is not in the numbers themselves, but in the fact that the benefits are used in the executing portfolios or projects with no taught who came up with the idea and the associated costs. Theoretical this can be solved by sharing the business benefits, but in practise it usually turns out to be non existence, unless this is mentioned and agreed before starting the process.

3.4.2 Risk reduction

Capturing risk reduction is a more complicated task and will only work if the enterprise architects and other managers have done a good job in capturing the present risks before implementing the solution described in this chapter.

The main areas of risk reduction is in the fact of the reuse and fewer new components that usually will increase the risks and a risk reduction monitoring always needs to take all the overall risks as a combined value. The main risk reduction however will be in the much better cost prediction that the service catalogue will enable.

3.4.3 Faster time to market

A faster time to market is already archived through the creation of a service catalogue as solutions can be fitted together much faster and costs obtained.

Additional the strategy involving the market definition will focus the process of the portfolio and project management to deliver those Services really required by the customers instead of just the perceived ones.

4. Process execution and improvement of the IS processes

Corporation: An ingenious device for obtaining profit without individual responsibility.

Ambrose Bierce

4.1. Value

By describing and executing the IS processes the TCO is lowered in the same way as fixed process work saves money in all industries. Through process improvement or process maturity additionally the not so elegant processes that have required iterations in the past will be able to work without these iterations in the future and as such costs are saved.

By executing a described process with an audit function and constantly running through risk logging processes the overall risks will be dramatically diminished.

There is an argument that it will take longer to deliver if IS is following a strict process. This argument is the same argument that takes place in any industry where process driven work patterns are introduced. From experience in the area of process engineering there are usually two valid cases where following a process takes longer. The first one occurs if the process in question is overly complex and tries to answer all possibilities. The second valid case if a very senior person is working on the tasks. However on the assumption that the IS process is not overly complex and on the understanding that your IS department is not only full of the top IS people in your country, following a process in IS will improve the time to market.

4.2. Introduction

Most IS departments have very little in terms of a written down and lived process, actual I have NEVER experienced a single IS department with a full documented process of all functions in IS. Especial I have never seen any fully documented process that is mainly done by the CIO. On the other side in areas such as in finance we have clear processes and even often up to the CFO.

As IT or IS department we are usually bad at process work for ourselves, while insisting that every other area of the business follows processes. I have seen that this is mostly not down to apathy, but to the fact that we have too many frameworks and too many processes in the frameworks. The problem is just that the frameworks such as Prince 2, TOGAF, MSP. Six Sigma,... are good at describing their own area well but not very good in describing the overall process.

In chapter 2 I introduced the different motivations in Enterprise Architecture. It is now important to create a customised IS process in your IS department; so if you have a company that is principle based you want to introduce checks on principles between mayor tasks.

The aim of this book is also not to concentrate at all the processes in a given IS department, but to focus on those in the core architecture and design area. However all areas will be discussed and the details on the other processes can be accessed via the Critical Enterprise Architecture Netcast.

I have researched roughly 6 categories that IS Processes are currently described (they might be more), for each category I will offer a short description and then list the associated frameworks (mainly concentrate on European and Global frameworks as I am less familiar with Chinese, Russian or other frameworks in languages that I cannot understand):

Change centric focuses on readiness, project & programme management, methods, alignment and benefits

Frameworks associated are:

- Prince2

- PMBOK

- MSP

- MoR

- CMMI

- OPM3

- COBIT

IT strategy centric focuses on information strategy, business and IT architecture & IT principles

Frameworks associated are:

- TOGAF

- ITIL v3

- Balanced Scorecard

- Zachman

IT & business centric focuses on the human structural vs. market capital balance, organisational issues and business IT integration balance approach

Frameworks associated are:

- ◆ Balanced Scorecard

- ◆ ISO 38500

- ◆ Zachman

Risk & conformance centric focuses on governance, conformance, compliance, controls and risk management & compliance centric

Frameworks associated are:

- • COSO

- • CoBIT

- • Balanced Scorecard

- • ISO 38500

- • SOX

- • PCI DSS

- • ISO 27001

- Baldridge

Business centric focuses on business models, business environments and business strategies

Frameworks associated are:

- Six Sigma

- Balanced Scorecard

- Business Plans

- Strategic Plans

- TCO/ROI

- Green IT

Operations centric focus on business operations, IT operations, IT asset management, SLM and security

Frameworks associated are:

- Data Protection Acts

- CoBIT

- ITIL

- ITPO

- Six Sigma

- ◆ PCI DSS

- ◆ ISO 27001

- ◆ ISO 20000

- ◆ BCM

All trademarks or registered trademarks are the property of their respective owners.

The ideal IS process therefore needs to take all these different frameworks into considerations and ensure that the process is workable. This is why I started some years ago to combine all the lessons learnt from all the frameworks with the input from my previous work. I then started to implement a standard process with the individual input of the IS management and created a pragmatic IS process that is adoptable and workable in most enterprises.

I have divided the IS process in some level 1 processes such as strategy, portfolio management, project management, design and architecture, transition and service management. Within this book I will list the complete IS Level 2 & 3 in Appendix A for reference and I will introduce each Level 3 process in detail in the Critical Enterprise Architecture Netcast.

4.3. The detailed Enterprise Architecture process

Since this book only caries a limited space it is impossible to show and discuss all IS processes in detail. However I will run them all through in my Netcast.

Before going further I would like you to look at Appendix A where you can find them all at a high level description. In this chapter I will however concentrate mainly on the processes where enterprise architects are directly involved with the exception of the two first Level 2 processes described in the previous chapter. However it is true to say that all processes need to be described before all the value can be extracted.

I have created the details of the processes from as many frameworks as possible that still make sense for the value driven enterprise. However I will disappoint many that are used to a framework as reference. The main reason for not following any particular framework is the fact that they were not only written with a specific reason in mind, but that they are usually not taking the fact into consideration that IT is delivered as a team.

For this book I will only concentrate on the architecture & design process.

4.3.1 the IS (or IT) organisation in the enterprise

Organisation and processes are always closely related. It is possible to implement processes into any organisation to a certain point in maturity. However after trying to reach for a CMMI Level 3 it is important also to change the organisation into a format that at least will enforce the process ownership.

So for my explanations I have used the following organisational structure:

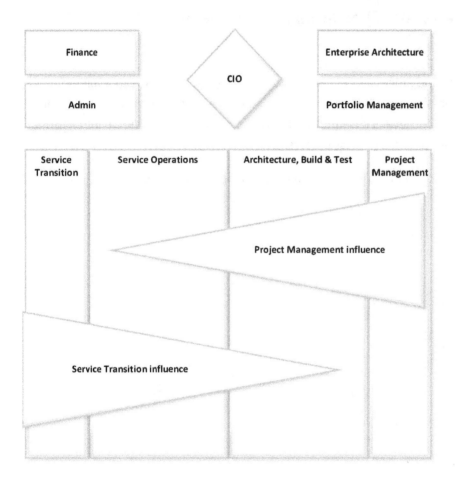

The boxes contain the functions, whereas the triangles describe the influence in term of a matrix management.

I have deliberately chosen this simplified format as it presents the minimum of necessary function in IS. Even if the functions at a very small enterprise might be covered with the same persons.

In essence every IS department has a CIO, staff functions and 4 departments for specific tasks.

The staff functions are for the enterprise wide tasks:

- Portfolio Management

- Enterprise Architecture

- IT finance and budgets

- Administration

The closely associated processes are the strategy and the portfolio processes. However the staff will work on many other processes. In the case of administration and finance these are not even contained in the IS processes, but mainly in the processes discussed in the next chapter.

The specific departments on the other hand are:

- Project Management for managing any projects

- Service Transition for release and change management, as well as service improvements

- Service Operations to operate the Services

- Architecture, Build & Test for creating new Services

Project management only consists out of few people, but will use many resources from the Architecture, Build & Test team and few from Service Operations, whereas the service transition will use many resources from Service Operations and a few from the Architecture, Build & Test team.

This representation is of course deliberately crude to allow enterprise architects to deploy it in any size of enterprise.

4.3.2 The architecture & design process

Among the strategy and portfolio process in IS the architecture & design process is one of most important Level 1 processes in IT.

4.3.2.1 Business architecture

Business architecture is certainly the one area that is least best described in any framework, the most that is usually described is a better kind of business analysis, maybe with a bit of a comment on non functional requirements (NFR) that are called Service Level Requirements in a service environment. This in itself was one of the reasons I started to document enterprise architecture as this constantly annoyed me.

Since the service orientation requires not only requires a business architecture, but a service orientated business architecture I am quite happy to start with this as the most important of all level 2 processes in architecture & design.

4.3.2.1.1 Define Business Objectives

The first process in business architecture will start very much in the same way that a good business analysis team do starting with the constraints such as budget & time, gather the drivers for change, get requirements, create the process thereof and represent it back. The definition of roles and responsibilities may also be included, whereas documentation on maturity and other initiatives is often forgotten. The maturity is key for a successful business architecture as with immature organisations you will quickly see that their requirements are just suggestions in a way, whereas mature organisations will really be able to tell you the real requirements. As a rule of thumb less mature organisation require more mature business architects. This in itself is also a main reason that many IS deliverables are pretty useless to the users even if they deliver the exact requirements. Other initiatives also have an influence on the business architecture, however if your enterprise is pressed on time this part and its associated risk is partially mitigated by the service based approach in itself. The main important reason to capture this is to map the interdependencies of the Services themselves.

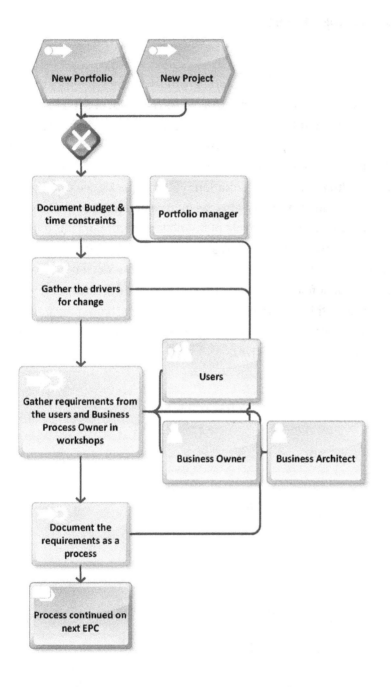

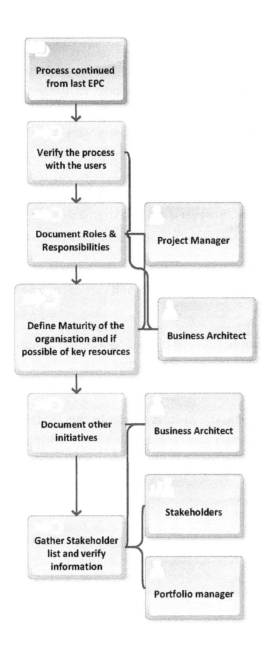

Process continued from last EPC

Verify the process with the users

Document Roles & Responsibilities

Project Manager

Define Maturity of the organisation and if possible of key resources

Business Architect

Document other initiatives

Business Architect

Stakeholders

Gather Stakeholder list and verify information

Portfolio manager

4.3.2.1.2 Develop Priorities

Within any enterprise on any protect or portfolio you will always find the problems on priorities. In a perfect world this would not be so, because you would ask the sponsor or business owner and get a good answer. In reality you will find that everything is top priority, which does not help once you have to make choices on versioning or if the budget is cut. This is why in the business architecture I will use the same priorities mentioned in chapter 3 on a value based approach (legal, strategic, financial, risk & competitive) so that we can determine the true factors behind this. This process can be eliminated if it is a very mature organisation. However they are extremely rare in my experience.

One has to get the information from various sources, so the competitive factors for example can only be determined by association with products and services and by looking at the KPI's.

Some steps in the process are or should not be done by the business architect, but by the portfolio manager as he/she should already know this (see portfolio management processes in the Netcast).

A very important artefact that is determined in this process (or ideally should already be in existence) is the risk reward matrix as this graph will highlight the risks understood and the rewards expected and should be used throughout the entire life cycle as a reference document.

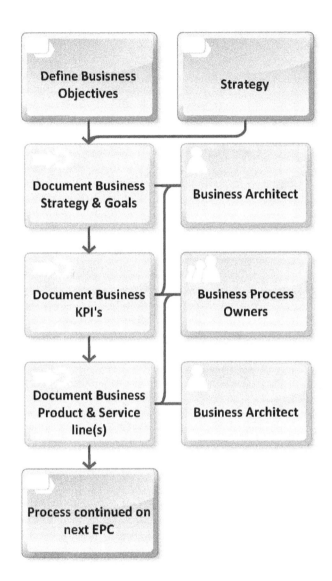

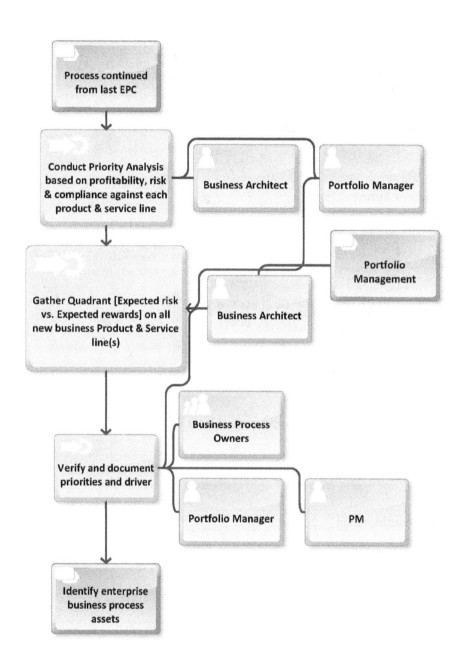

Process continued from last EPC

Conduct Priority Analysis based on profitability, risk & compliance against each product & service line

Business Architect

Portfolio Manager

Portfolio Management

Gather Quadrant [Expected risk vs. Expected rewards] on all new business Product & Service line(s)

Business Architect

Business Process Owners

Verify and document priorities and driver

Portfolio Manager

PM

Identify enterprise business process assets

4.3.2.1.3 Identify enterprise business process assets

Once a business process is created and signed off, only half of the work is done. The business process is always associated with many supporting requirements and objectives. It is very important that all of these are discovered early in the process to ensure that the project is not wasting to much time in running in blind alleys or that even SLR's and consequently SLA's are drafted in the wrong way. Another reason is to ensure the customer satisfaction.

A classical example where this process is imminent important is the Hire-to-Retire business process (or the HR process), as there are many legal considerations in this process.

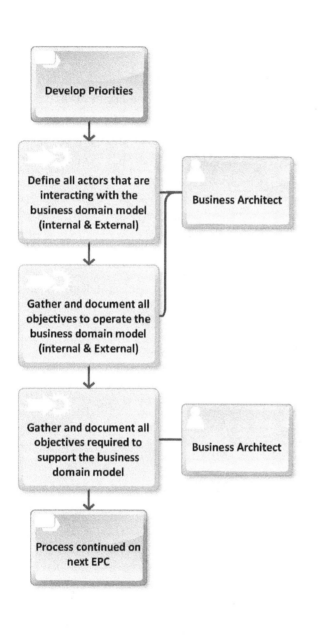

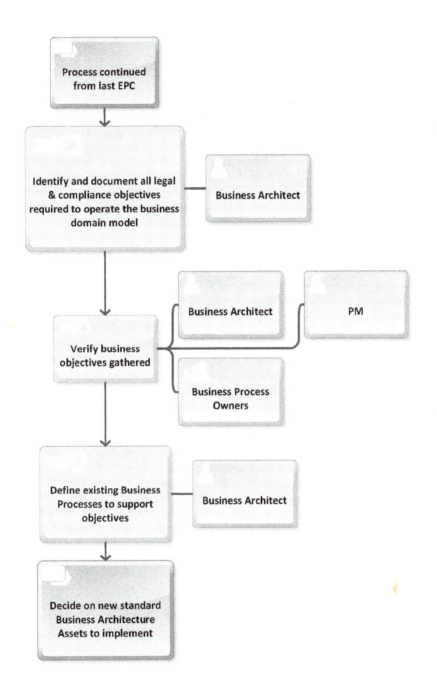

4.3.2.1.4 Decide on new standard business architecture assets to implement

After looking at the requirements and associated information the next step is to create the Target Business Process Model (TBPM) by analysing the requirements and the suggested business process against best practices and also determine a reuse of an existing business process in the enterprise. This step is where the business architecture gets fundamental different to the traditional business analysis.

It is important to understand that most business owners are not aware of the things happening in other departments of the enterprise. So this is why we need to identify the business process reuse long time before we reach any solution architecture as it may turn out that solution architecture is not needed at all. This is also the reason why this step should not be skipped.

The industry best practices should be used as described in chapter 5 of this book.

It should be pointed out that most business owners are quite glad if it turns out that their process is not as unique as thought as this means less work for them and a de-risking of their area; as it is likely that someone else already tried out all the inherent traps in a new process.

It is of course also important to link all the business process assets that were gathered in the last chapter into the TBPM.

Finally it is important also to add the priorities to the TBPM to create a Target Value Business Process that contains the drivers toward value and will in itself already lead towards the service level requirements (SLR) to priorities the right Services instead of doing the traditional Non Functional Agreement where all parts of the business process supporting IS Services are handled in the same way.

The Business Architecture roadmap should then also contain a chapter on opportunities to reuse this service for another part of the enterprise or clearly state why this is not feasible. The goal in the architecture processes is always to detect reuse as soon as possible to reduce costs and risks and to shorten the delivery time. Once the process is implemented it becomes obvious that the process is not a time consumer but rather the opposite if implemented in the right way.

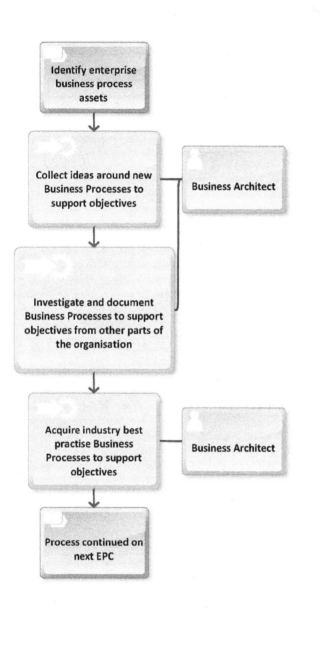

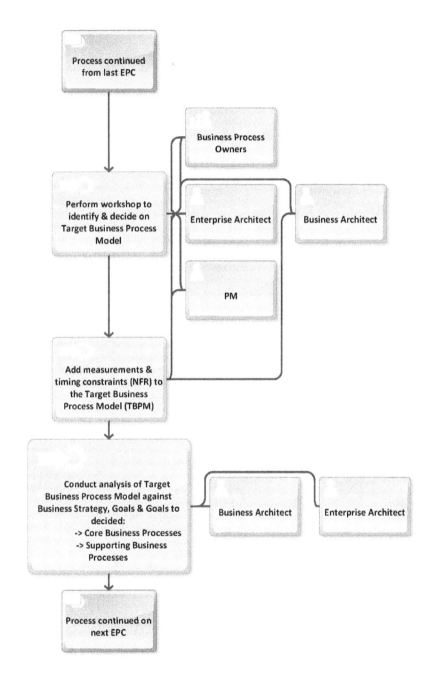

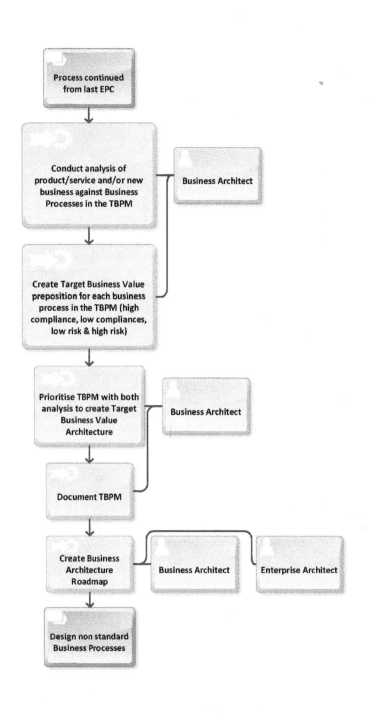

4.3.2.1.5 Design non standard business processes

Like in technology architecture it is important in business architecture to treat anything that can not be constructed as reuse in a very sceptical way.

The main reason for not overusing this process is to introduce the cultural shift from processes and requirements as god given towards an enterprise or business architecture exercise. It is important not to point out the inherent flaw in the existing system, but to replace the missing knowledge on process reuse with one of knowledge. This in itself is also one of the key reasons that this book is full of process descriptions and will encourage the reader to listen to the Netcast of the author to discover even more on process knowledge.

An example of process reuse of two very different business areas is the implementation of a pharmaceutical production process in steel production. In the first moment there is no correlation on the processes. However once the processes are understood it is amazing how similar the processes are. There are the standard production tasks, but then you find that both processes have similar quality control, both require a lot management process and both are cutting a certain percentage of output off in the beginning and at the end of production as there are often chemical unbalances in the beginning and at the end. This process is also a good exercise in training to spot a process reuse.

This is why it is important not only to design the TBPM on bespoke processes, but also to ensure that the uniqueness is constantly rechecked. The goal has to be to reuse processes as much as possible so that many projects will stop at this phase in the architecture. Otherwise the traditional process is just followed without realising the real value benefit of enterprise architecture.

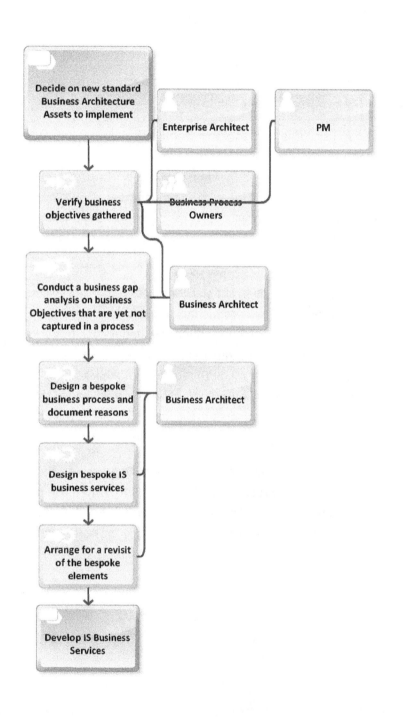

4.3.2.1.6 Develop business services

Only if the processes cannot be reused it is important to create IS business services matching the new processes. Here it is important that all information is entered in the service catalogue.

The outcome of the process is used by many different other processes as input, so this why it is important that the work is done up to a very high quality standard.

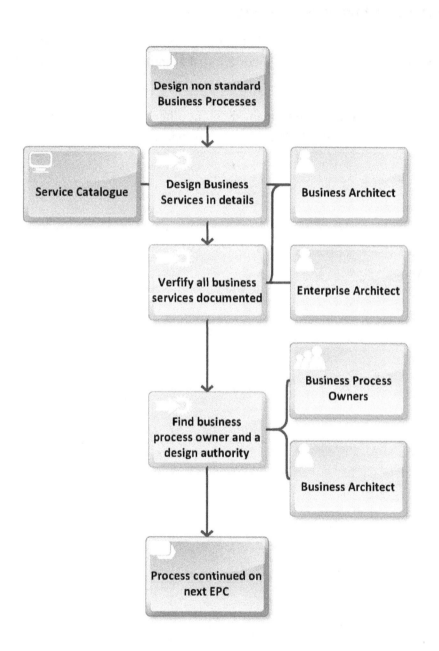

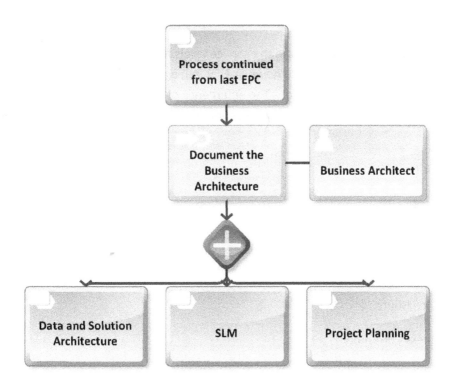

4.3.2.2 Service Level Management (create)

This Level 2 process is looking to create the service levels for any services. Traditionally in enterprise architecture the SLR were known as NFR, but again always with a wide list of what should be included and what not. The emergence of Service Management as a parallel process has done very much good in defining what is included in the Service Levels as:

- ✓ Security
- ✓ Capacity
- ✓ Availability
- ✓ Uptime
- ✓ Service Hours
- ✓ Business Continuity
- ✓ Reaction time
- ✓ Problem Response Time
- ✓ Incident Response Time

There are of course some other important factors around the service management such as suppliers, Design Authorities, value of the service and the service life cycle, but they can not really be described as Levels, rather more as Service Master Data.

There is a long debate as to the decision whether service management should belong into service operation or into the architecture & design domain; key here is to separate the creation of SLR and SLA minus any OLA (operational Level Agreements) on one hand from the ongoing management. Once you operate under this separation the debate is solved very fast. Within the Architecture & Design Level 1 process we are only looking at the "create" part of the Service Level Management.

To try to create a service based approach without the SLM process has to fail, as many of the defining objectives that drive IS Business Services and IS Services are contained in the service levels and they certainly also have a large influence on costs as well as designs.

Another note is also very important to mention here. SLM takes place between the business and the solution & data architecture. So that is why the SLM process will run in parallel with those processes. Even some of the SLM processes are interrelated, which sometimes makes the SLM process a bit murky. So please **DO NOT** use the processes in chronological order!

It should also be noted that it is very seldom that all processes in SLM are required.

4.3.2.2.1 Understand financial, legal and competitive factors

The first process in SLM is mainly a rehash of the "Develop Priorities" in business architecture. However the process that mainly involves the enterprise architect once it is decided that there is need for a new service will lock at the various factors much more in detail and involve a close link to the IS strategy. Additional the factors will now be checked with the various enterprise offices to get a high degree of accountability and accuracy.

At the end of the process the enterprise architect will therefore have to challenge the Project Manager on all the Financials and the Legal & Compliance factors. The process is mainly in place for the governance and should not hinder the progress of any project.

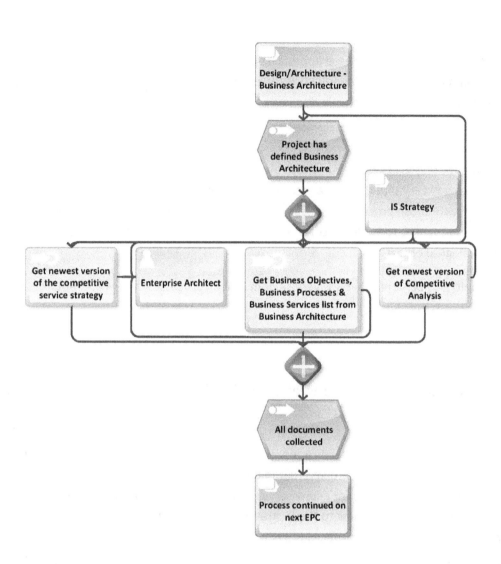

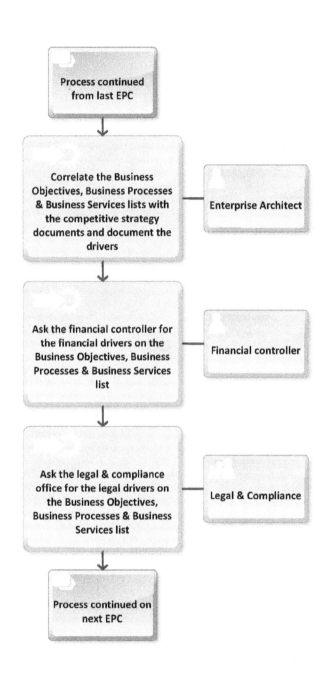

Process continued from last EPC

Correlate the Business Objectives, Business Processes & Business Services lists with the competitive strategy documents and document the drivers

Enterprise Architect

Ask the financial controller for the financial drivers on the Business Objectives, Business Processes & Business Services list

Financial controller

Ask the legal & compliance office for the legal drivers on the Business Objectives, Business Processes & Business Services list

Legal & Compliance

Process continued on next EPC

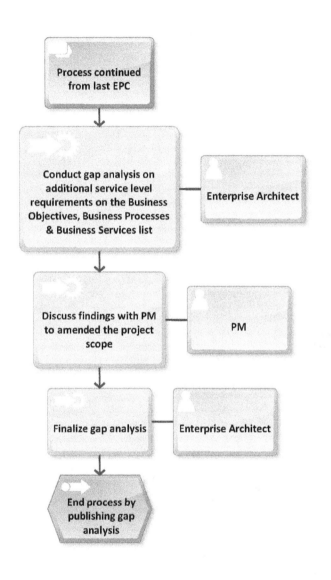

4.3.2.2.2 Understand KPI for higher management

The second process in SLM is very similar to the first one, with the exception that this time there is a check and further refinements of the business architecture against the key performance indicators (KPI) and the critical success factors (CSF).

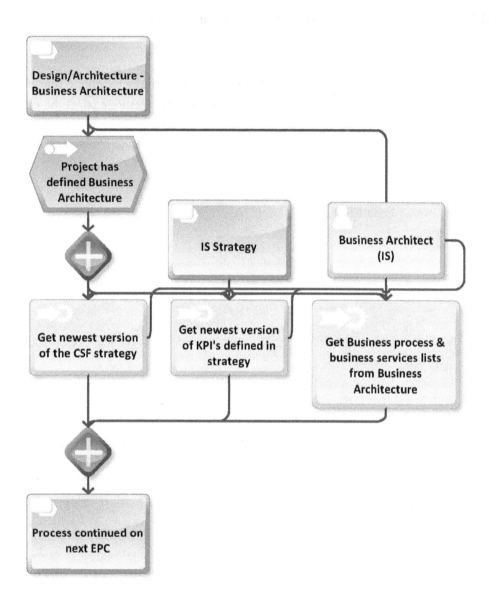

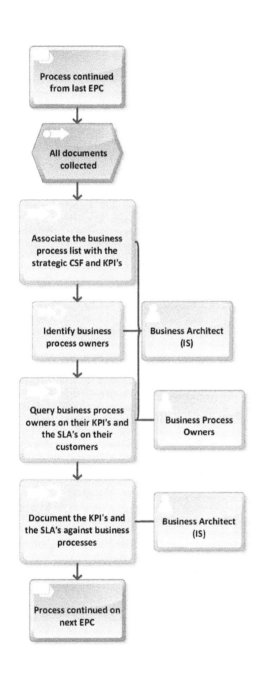

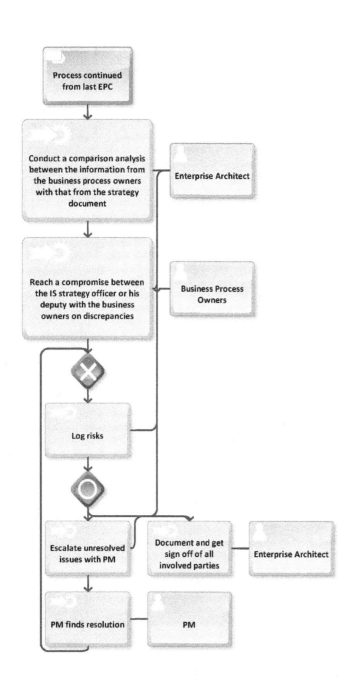

4.3.2.2.3 Draw SLA drafts

After the preliminary work the real process of drawing up the draft SLA starts. This process requires that some other processes that I have deliberately put in the further chapters are finished. These are the formulating of the service level requirements. However during the last years when I have implemented the process I have usually noticed that anyone familiar with the SLM process will understand the importance of the creation of services better when being presented with this process that will document the outcome. This is special true when looking at some infrastructure IS Services, as the architect involved first need to understand that by capturing the architecture the work is not done.

This process will focus on getting the detailed requirement analysis on the service level requirements (which after the previous work invested should not pose a large problem) and then suggest the relating SLA details. This process also involves the highest number of different staff as there are so many areas in SLM to consider. This is why the most important role in this process is that of the service manager, who is also ultimately responsible for the services.

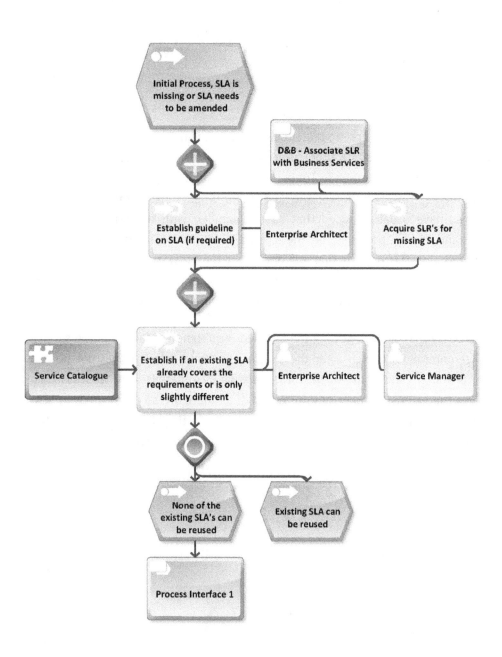

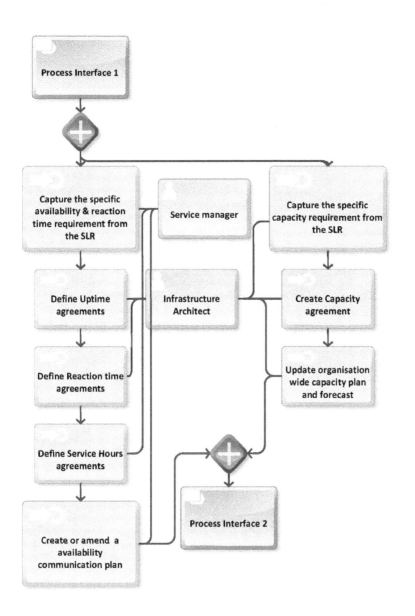

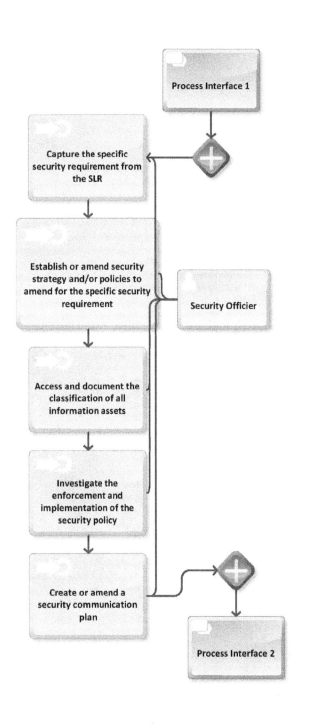

Process Interface 1

Capture the specific security requirement from the SLR

Establish or amend security strategy and/or policies to amend for the specific security requirement

Security Officier

Access and document the classification of all information assets

Investigate the enforcement and implementation of the security policy

Create or amend a security communication plan

Process Interface 2

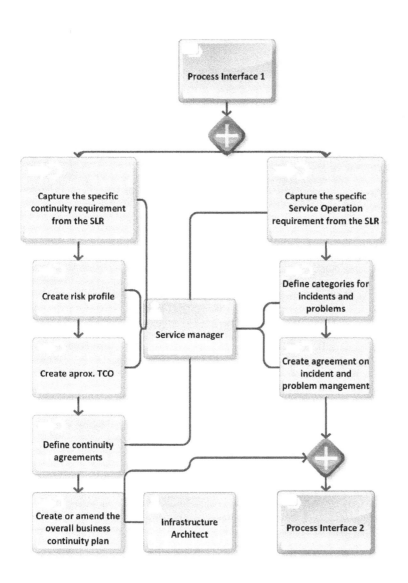

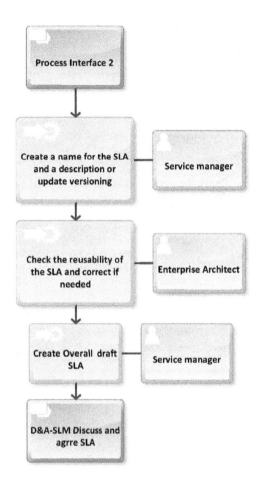

4.3.2.2.4 Discuss and agree SLA

The process for agreeing the SLA should be done last. Usually this process even if it seems short can often take a long time mainly if SLM is a new process.

The important fact on SLA's is to remember that not every new Service requires a new SLA unless the SLA's are written in a too specific way. So it is important to formulate SLA's that a more generic, which is one of the governance responsibilities of the enterprise architect during the stakeholder meeting.

It should also be noted that once an IS Services has more than one SLA associated with it, it is important to clone it and create a new service.

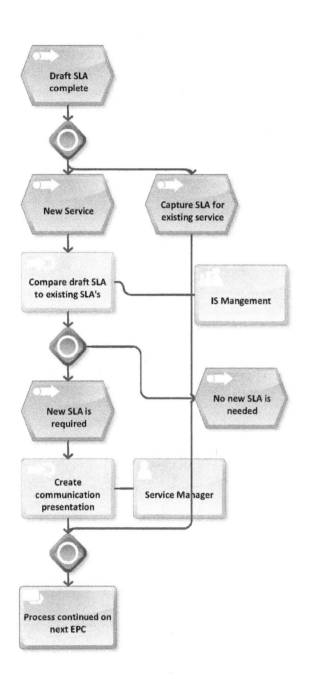

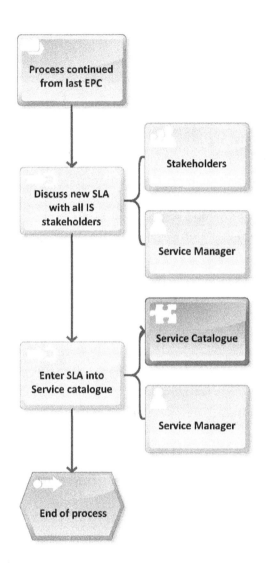

4.3.2.2.5 Budget for SLR's in business services

Within this process the financial implications of assigning certain SLR are calculated. It is normal in most organisations that the business owner first wants the best in term of SLR, until she/he realises how much it will cost. At that point it often goes the other way. This situation is just like in every business dealings were a product is configured (like buying a car and discover that even the paint is not included in the price), so this is why this process may occur in iterations.

It is important to point out that any supplier quoted at this point is just for cost determination and can be changed later under the assumption that the costs remain the same.

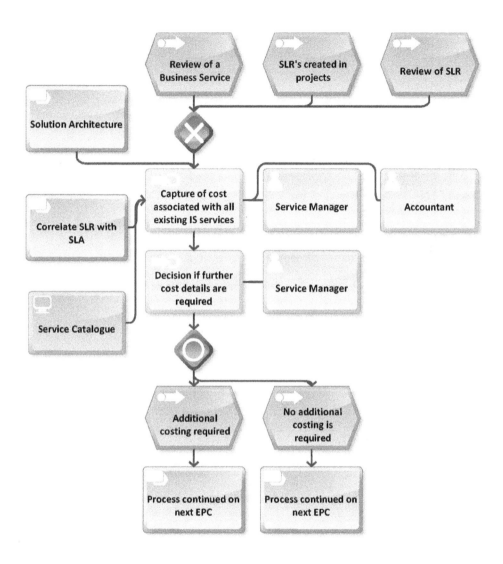

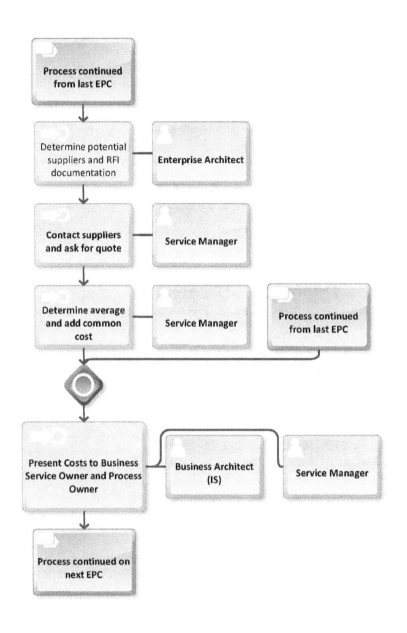

Process continued
from last EPC

Determine potential
suppliers and RFI
documentation

Enterprise Architect

Contact suppliers
and ask for quote

Service Manager

Determine average
and add common
cost

Service Manager

Process continued
from last EPC

Present Costs to Business
Service Owner and Process
Owner

Business Architect
(IS)

Service Manager

Process continued on
next EPC

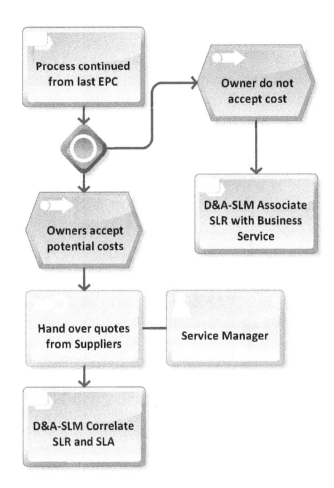

4.3.2.2.6 Create plan for SLM

This is a vital process that can or should not be passed, as it determines the suppliers of services and determines the service life cycle. Apart from this it also rechecks existing services and prepares the project to be transitioned into service operations. So even if a project is fully reusing existing business processes and IS services with only a change in configuration management this process still need to take place.

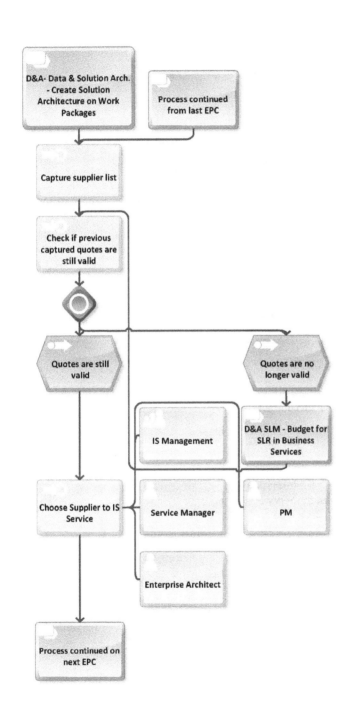

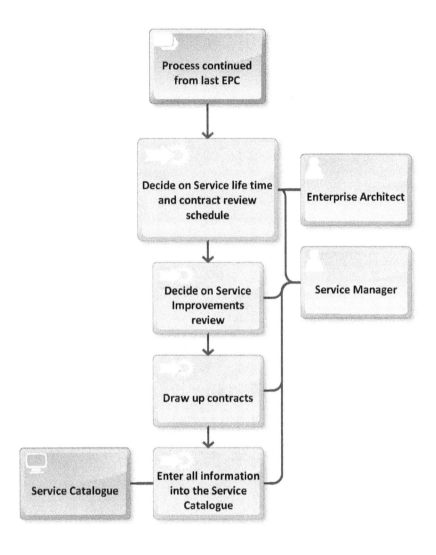

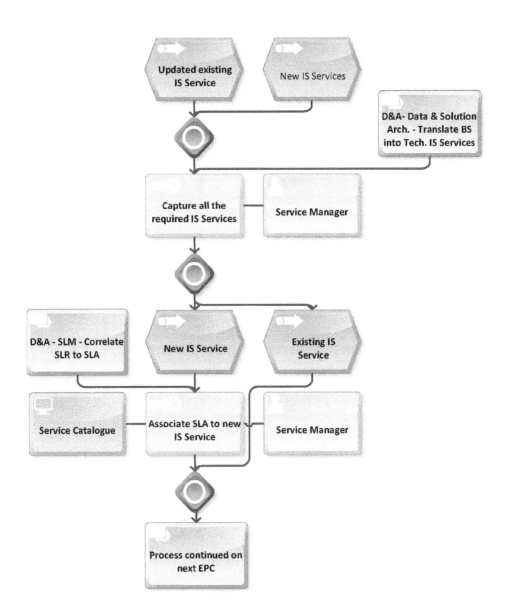

4.3.2.3 Data and solution architecture

Entering the data and solution architecture there are often two things that will happen if introducing the value based enterprise architecture. The first is Hubris and an ignorance of anything new. The second is that most solution architects will resent any process. This is special to solution architects even if they are often the ones that will constantly call for more process to happen. Solution architects are often most prone to create new templates and processes by just ignoring their own best advice at the next project. In my experience the only other role in IS with that much resistance on following a process is the CIO. This is why for the solution architect it is the best to combine his/her bonus to the process maturity if possible. The first 5 processes in this Level 2 process are the core ones that are required for SLM to do their work.

4.3.2.3.1 Translate business services into technical services as solution architecture

This process is one of the big ones. The process requires being started parallel with the three following data related processes and can only be finished when the data architecture is resolved. This solution architecture process will only work in a Service orientated way. At one point Services are split in Level 1 to 6. For reference please see chapter 3 of this book, however the solution and data architecture covers the Level 1 and 2, while the other levels are covered by Infrastructure or Technical Architects. The process in itself will always focus on the values set out in chapter one, namely, save costs through reuse, reduce and record risks and speed up the time to market. Another key feature is to check for cross dependencies and not only to look for low hanging fruits, but instead concentrate on a total quality insurance on the solution.

It should also be noted that skipping the data architectural processes will not help to accelerate the time to market.

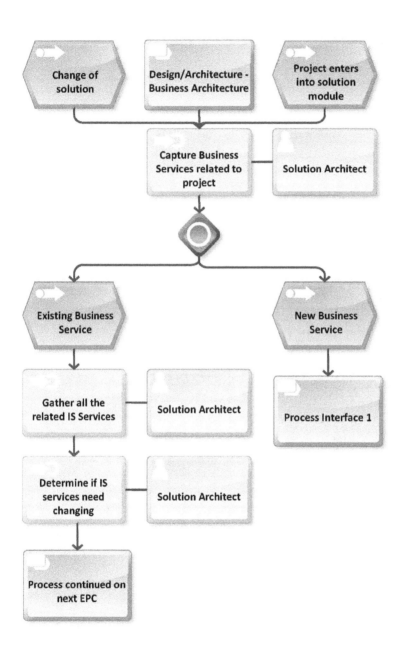

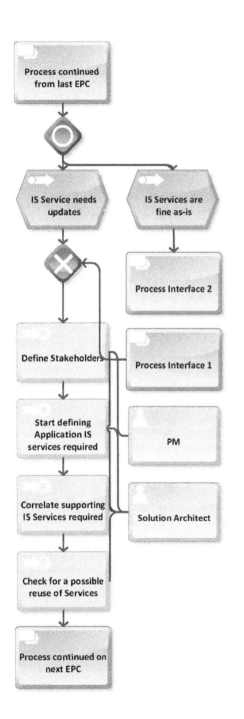

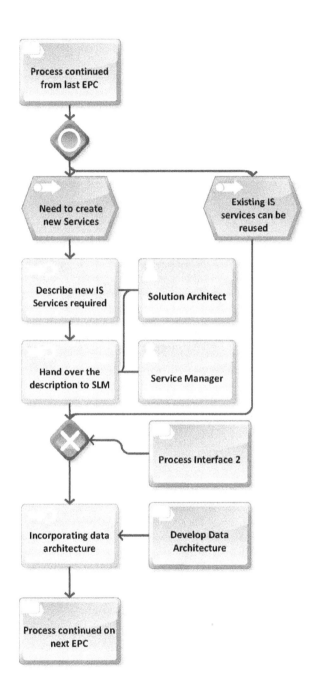

Process continued
from last EPC

Need to create
new Services

Existing IS
services can be
reused

Describe new IS
Services required

Solution Architect

Hand over the
description to SLM

Service Manager

Process Interface 2

Incorporating data
architecture

Develop Data
Architecture

Process continued on
next EPC

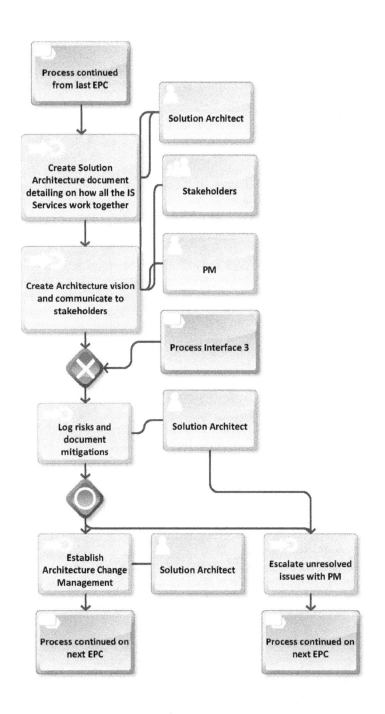

Process continued from last EPC

Create Solution Architecture document detailing on how all the IS Services work together

Solution Architect

Create Architecture vision and communicate to stakeholders

Stakeholders

PM

Process Interface 3

Log risks and document mitigations

Solution Architect

Establish Architecture Change Management

Solution Architect

Escalate unresolved issues with PM

Process continued on next EPC

Process continued on next EPC

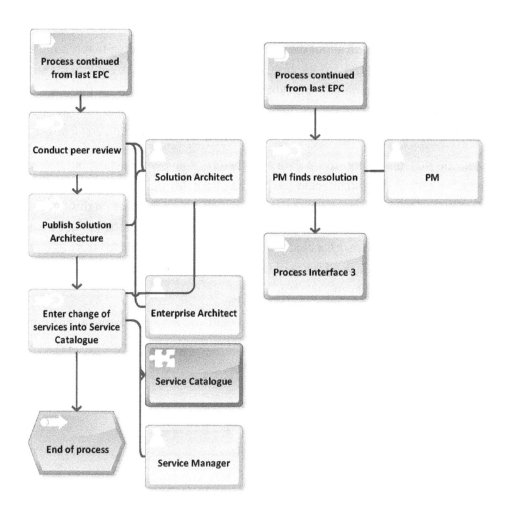

4.3.2.3.2 Create data requirements

This and the next process is all about data architecture, which is an area that is not well covered in a service orientated architecture, as data is not prone to be cut into the service concept. That said it is even more important to do the data architecture within the process to the highest quality level possible. Given the fact that the enterprise will move into more and more maturity on theses processes, this will help the data architecture.

I personally do NOT see an enterprise data architecture as an own function, but only see the need of an explicit data architect in the project phase. My opinion is mainly influenced by the fact that I have never been able to come up with a business case on this topic. Even if you ignore the missing cost aspect all indications show that neither the risk nor the time to market can be reduced by such a central function. The main reason for this can be found in the fact that data in itself is not of importance, but only the requirements make data valuable or other data even valueless.

So if you start organising data without the end in sight you may just do the wrong thing. That said it is still important to maintain the central enterprise data repository for the data structure, the data classification and how it is handled.

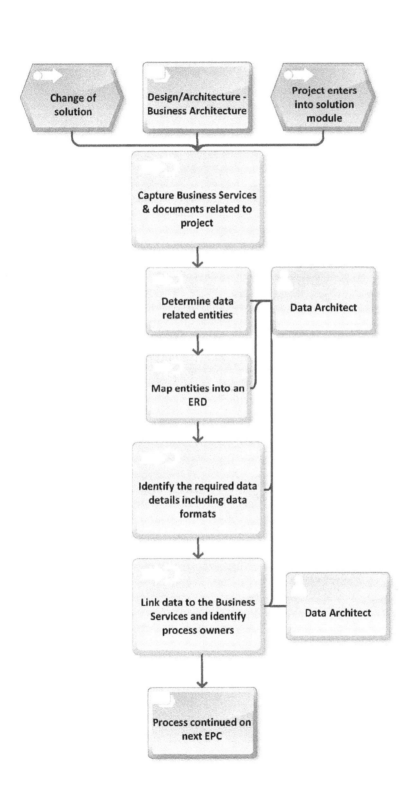

Change of solution

Design/Architecture - Business Architecture

Project enters into solution module

Capture Business Services & documents related to project

Determine data related entities

Data Architect

Map entities into an ERD

Identify the required data details including data formats

Link data to the Business Services and identify process owners

Data Architect

Process continued on next EPC

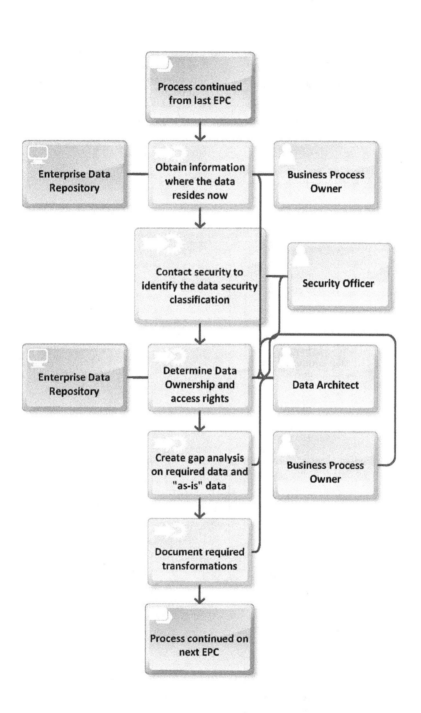

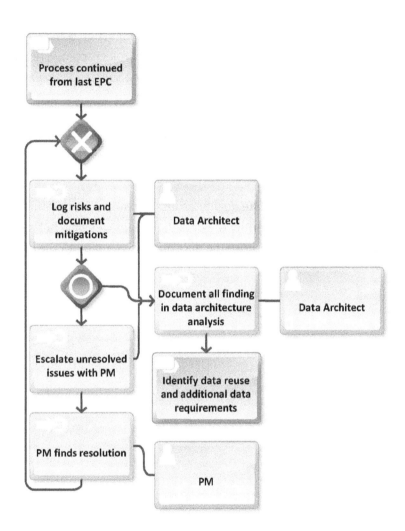

4.3.2.3.3 Identify data reuse and additional data requirements

In this crucial process that is often not even thought about, the first action is to identify the data suppliers. By doing this it sometimes turns out that the project scope is required to be widened or changed as the data sometimes is required to be sourced from external sources.

The next group of tasks is to determine how to handle existing data. Here it is important to determine the subject on data ownership, data migration, data sanity and data interdependencies.

Then the process will concentrate on the data quality issues. This step does not only need a close partnership with the business to identify the data that needs cleaning, but also determine a process to ensure that in the future the data quality is kept up to the highest level.

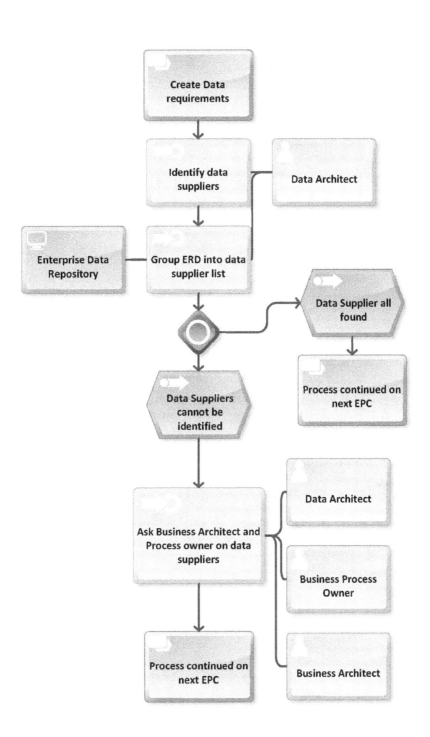

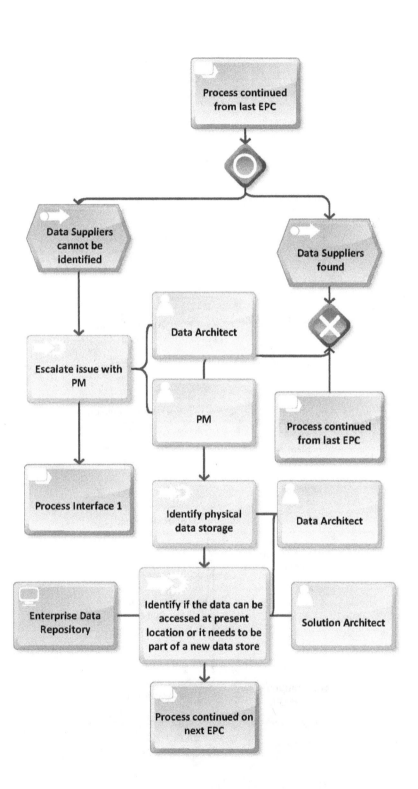

Process continued from last EPC

Data Suppliers cannot be identified

Data Suppliers found

Data Architect

Escalate issue with PM

PM

Process continued from last EPC

Process Interface 1

Identify physical data storage

Data Architect

Enterprise Data Repository

Identify if the data can be accessed at present location or it needs to be part of a new data store

Solution Architect

Process continued on next EPC

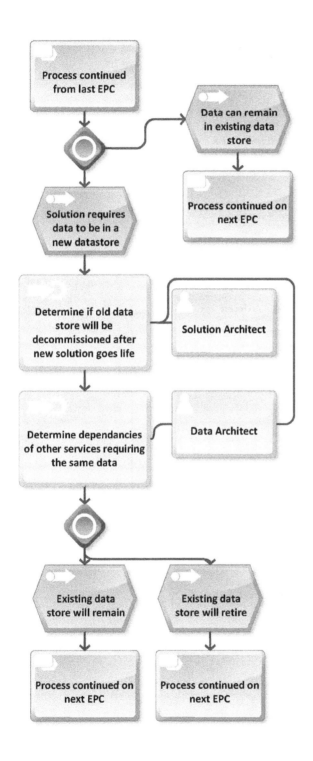

Process continued from last EPC

Data can remain in existing data store

Process continued on next EPC

Solution requires data to be in a new datastore

Determine if old data store will be decommissioned after new solution goes life

Solution Architect

Determine dependancies of other services requiring the same data

Data Architect

Existing data store will remain

Existing data store will retire

Process continued on next EPC

Process continued on next EPC

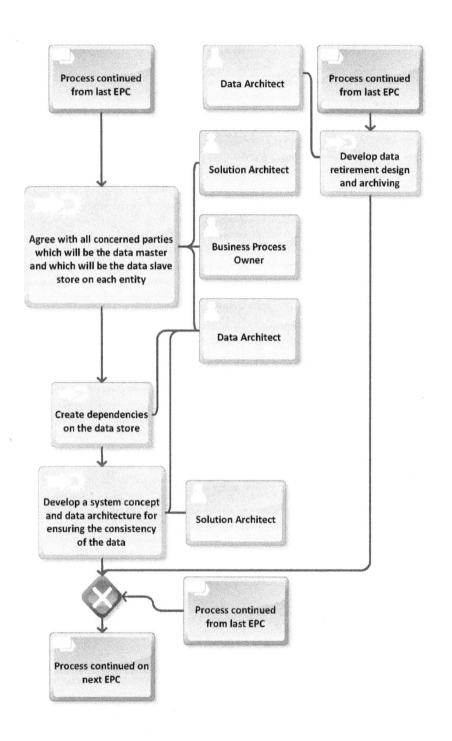

Process continued from last EPC

Data Architect

Process continued from last EPC

Solution Architect

Develop data retirement design and archiving

Agree with all concerned parties which will be the data master and which will be the data slave store on each entity

Business Process Owner

Data Architect

Create dependencies on the data store

Develop a system concept and data architecture for ensuring the consistency of the data

Solution Architect

Process continued from last EPC

Process continued on next EPC

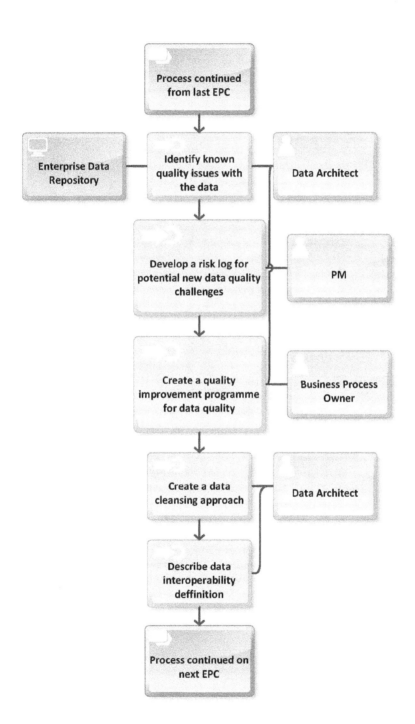

Process continued from last EPC

Enterprise Data Repository

Identify known quality issues with the data

Data Architect

Develop a risk log for potential new data quality challenges

PM

Create a quality improvement programme for data quality

Business Process Owner

Create a data cleansing approach

Data Architect

Describe data interoperability deffinition

Process continued on next EPC

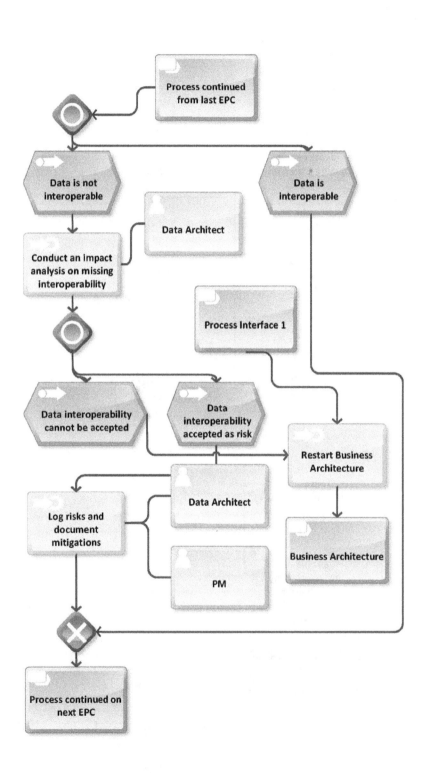

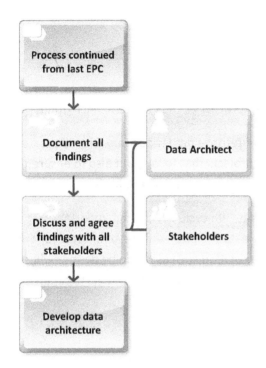

4.3.2.3.4 Develop Data Architecture

This process needs to happen together with the "Translate Business Services into Technical Services as Solution Architecture" process as they relate to each other.

The process first takes care to update the enterprise data repository with all the information gathered so far to benefit the projects that follow, but also to ensure that other project are not destroying the data integrity of the present project.

The second main task is to determine the data life cycle which is an important step that it will reduce further costs on the solution as data will often only be of interest for the business (e.g. orders) for a limited time. Legislation such as retaining periods will also need to be taken into this consideration as in some countries it is illegal to retain data past a defined moment in time.

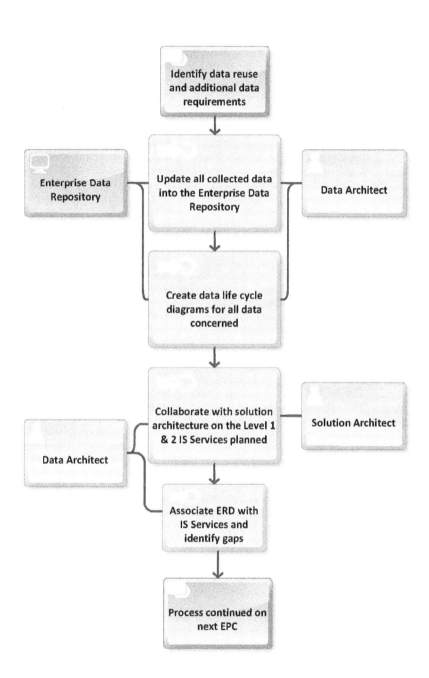

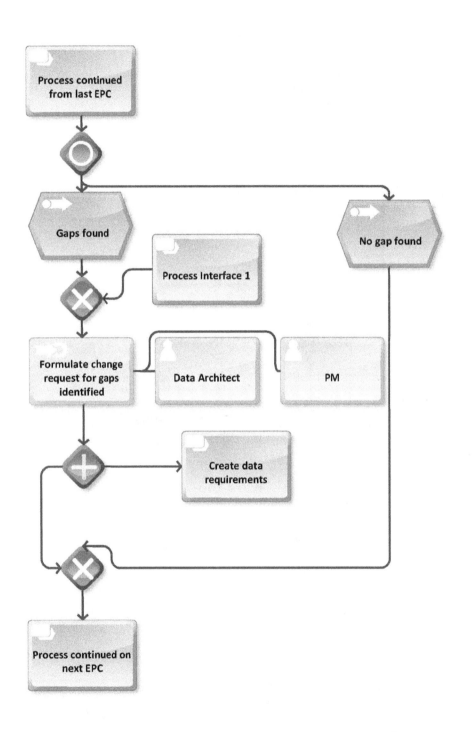

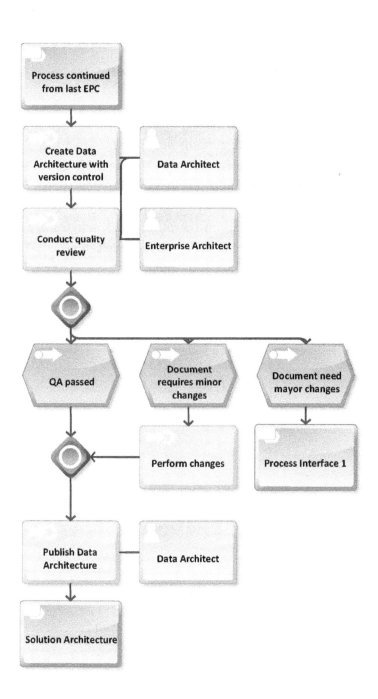

4.3.2.3.5 Create solution architecture on work packages

After finishing the core data and solution architecture the next step is to split the work into packages and as such enable the project managers to take the project further. To do this it is important to engage potential suppliers in this preparation, as any work package should always be constructed in a way that on one hand it has the least amount of interdependencies and on the other hand requires a minimum of parties working together to reduce the risk of miscommunication.

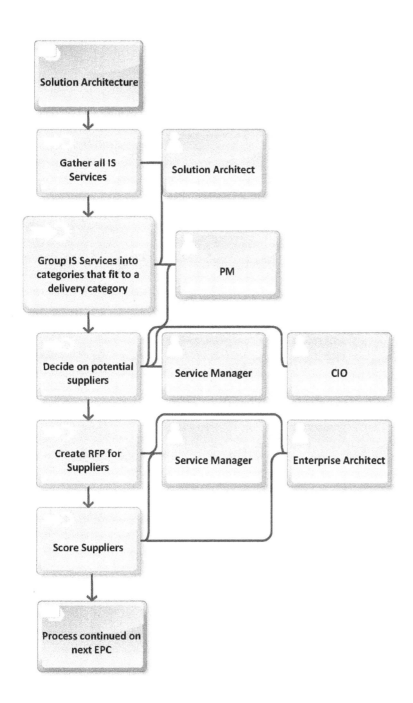

Solution Architecture

Gather all IS Services — **Solution Architect**

Group IS Services into categories that fit to a delivery category — **PM**

Decide on potential suppliers — **Service Manager** — **CIO**

Create RFP for Suppliers — **Service Manager** — **Enterprise Architect**

Score Suppliers

Process continued on next EPC

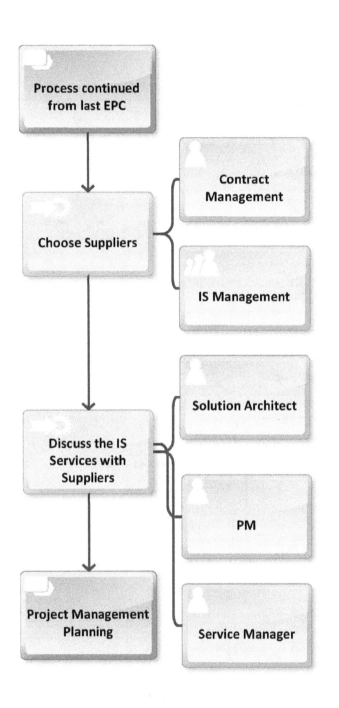

4.3.2.3.6 Integrate SLM into solution architectures

Before starting the designs the integration with Service Level Management has to be undertaken to ensure that all the Service Levels are well understood by the suppliers. This process should be done in a very short period, if it is managed well.

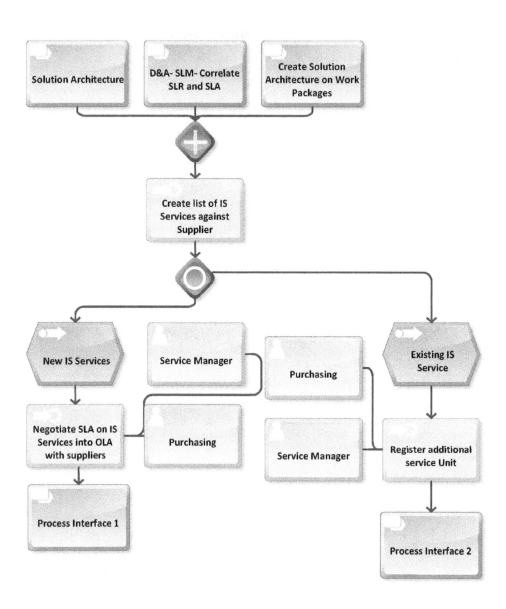

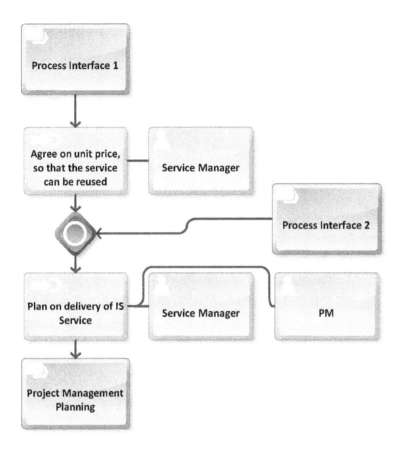

Process Interface 1

Agree on unit price, so that the service can be reused

Service Manager

Process Interface 2

Plan on delivery of IS Service

Service Manager

PM

Project Management Planning

4.3.2.3.7 Create designs

After the data & solution architecture is done all the designs will need to be worked on; this process will involve many specialists and therefore needs to be managed well.

The first step is to create a logic view on how all the Services will interact and which group is responsible for what piece. In large projects it is important that this not left to a project manager alone unless you have a technical project manager on hand the solution architect is required to help him/her in the coordination.

The design phase as such is also the ideal point where to switch from a higher level solution and SLM design to the detailed one. This break point has two points of significances. The first one is purely for the project management as a gate point. Up to this point most of documentation will be in the form of documents and presentations that can be understood by a larger group. From this point onwards all documentation should follow standards such as UML, ERD, BPMN, etc. This way it will be possible to also stop the endless discussions on notations on high level designs. Again apart from the service catalogue and the enterprise data repository I can not see the value in another enterprise wide repository as I tried many times unsuccessful to create a ROI case for this.

At the end of the design process you as an enterprise architect should ensure that the designs are only reviewed by technical experts with the exception of the project manager, as I have seen to many projects were business people got invited, with the result that everything took much longer and the business user got often so frustrated of the "wasted" time that they could often only be persuaded very hard to return to UAT.

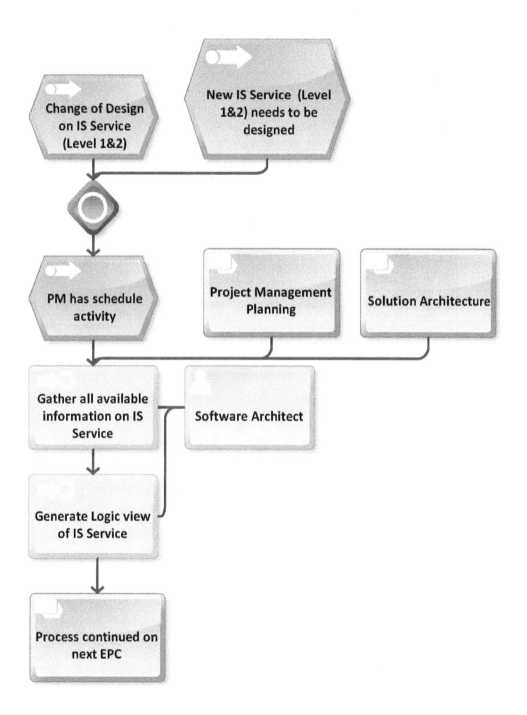

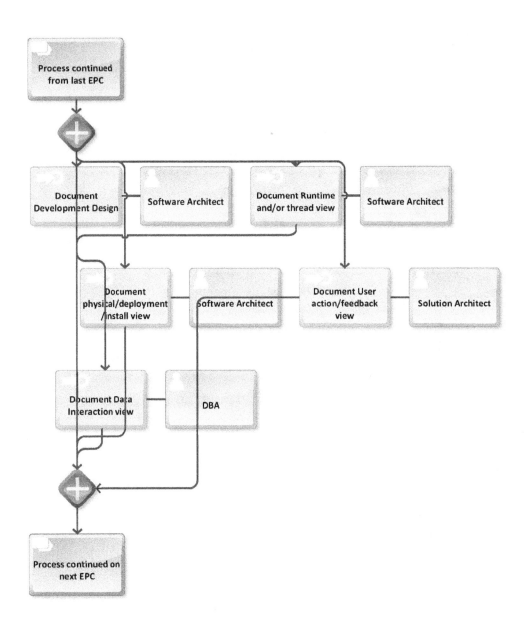

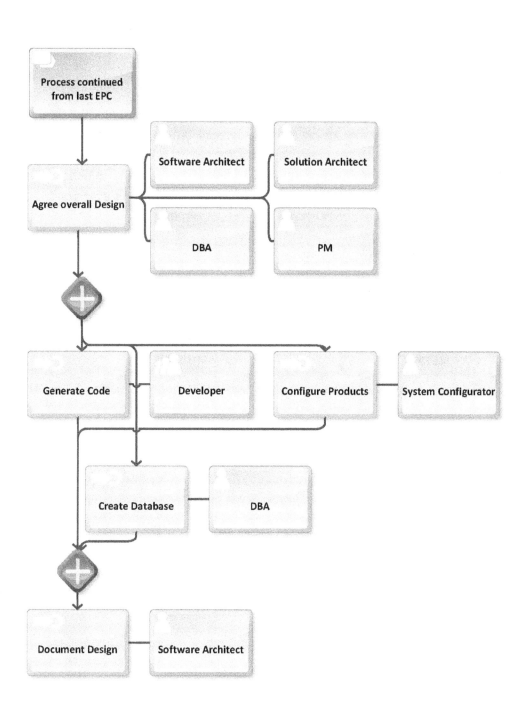

4.3.2.3.8 Create test plans and test scripts

After creating the solution architecture and before starting the development the test plans need to be written. Ideally some test scripts writing should take place earlier in terms of the V model, however in my experience it is more important that it is done together in a project setting and still well before the solution is build. It should be noted that it is a good idea not to linger to long on test strategy as this strategy will only need to cover the project in question.

A key element other than in the classical V model is the SLM Test to ensure that the services work against the given SLR.

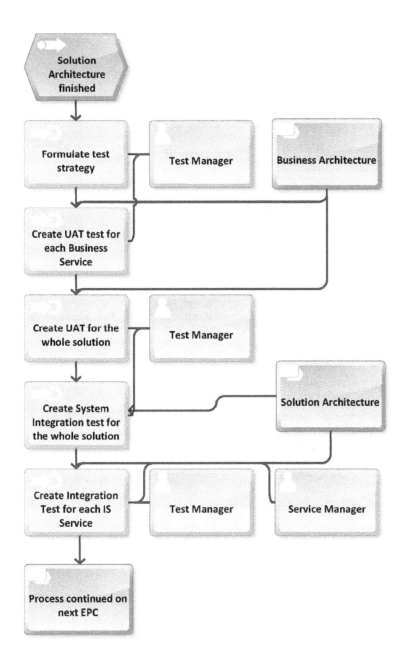

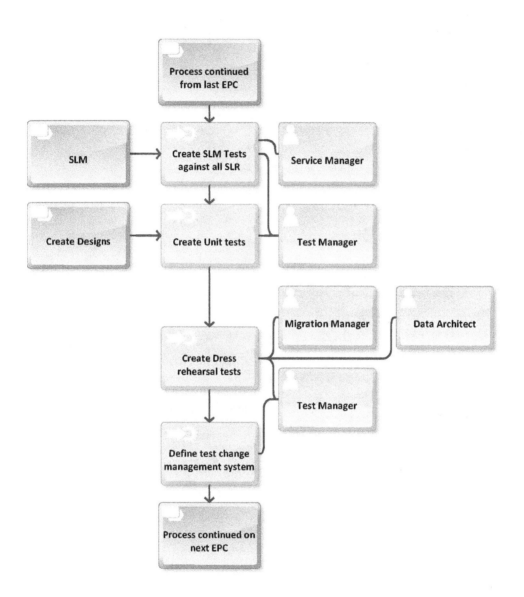

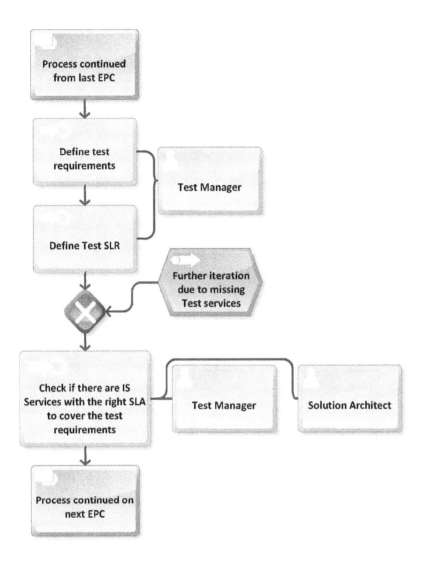

Process continued from last EPC

Define test requirements

Test Manager

Define Test SLR

Further iteration due to missing Test services

Check if there are IS Services with the right SLA to cover the test requirements

Test Manager

Solution Architect

Process continued on next EPC

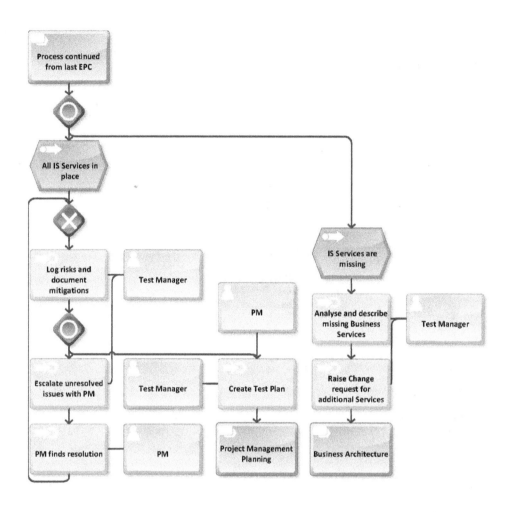

Process continued from last EPC

All IS Services in place

Log risks and document mitigations

Test Manager

PM

IS Services are missing

Analyse and describe missing Business Services

Test Manager

Escalate unresolved issues with PM

Test Manager

Create Test Plan

Raise Change request for additional Services

PM finds resolution

PM

Project Management Planning

Business Architecture

4.3.2.3.9 Identify opportunities

After finishing the solution architecture it is advisable to identify opportunities. This step of the wider process will focus the architecture on the wider enterprise picture.

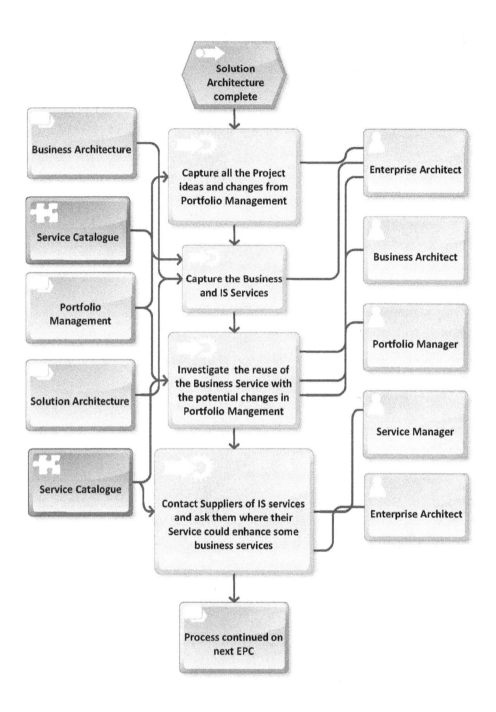

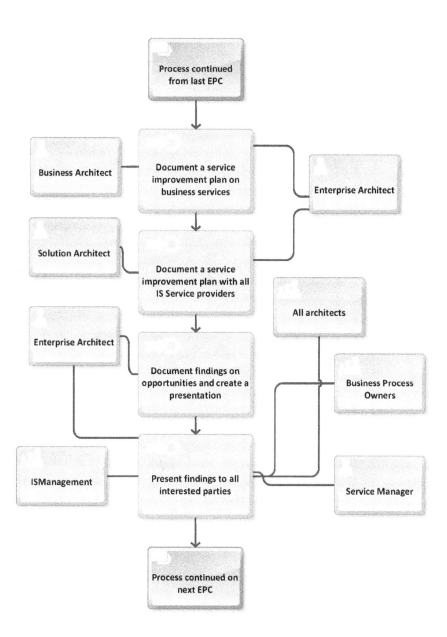

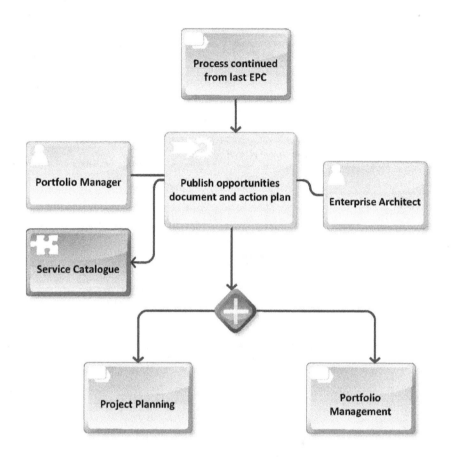

4.3.2.3.10 Design migrations

Unless the solution architecture is build on a green field without any previous systems in place migrations are always part of almost all projects. The important thing to remember at this point is that most of the work in defining the architecture was already done earlier in the process.

As you can see that this process involves very many tasks it is important to start this activity as early as possible and ensure that it is well resourced.

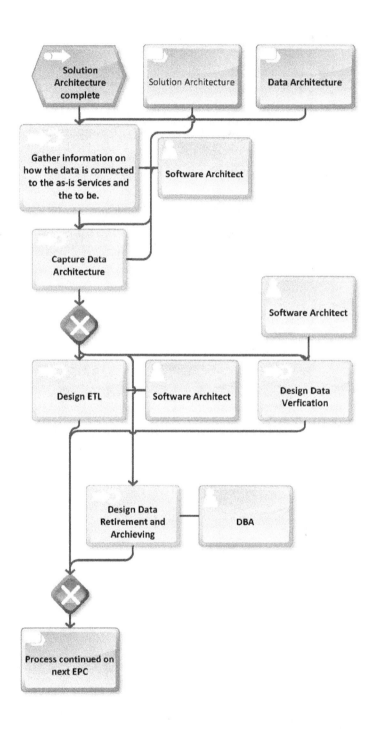

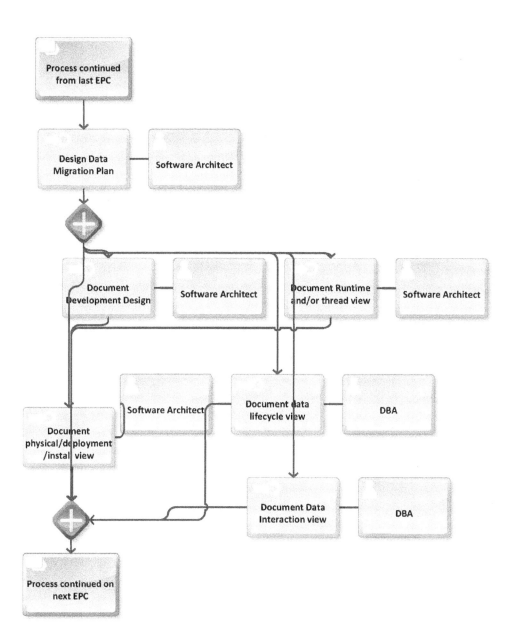

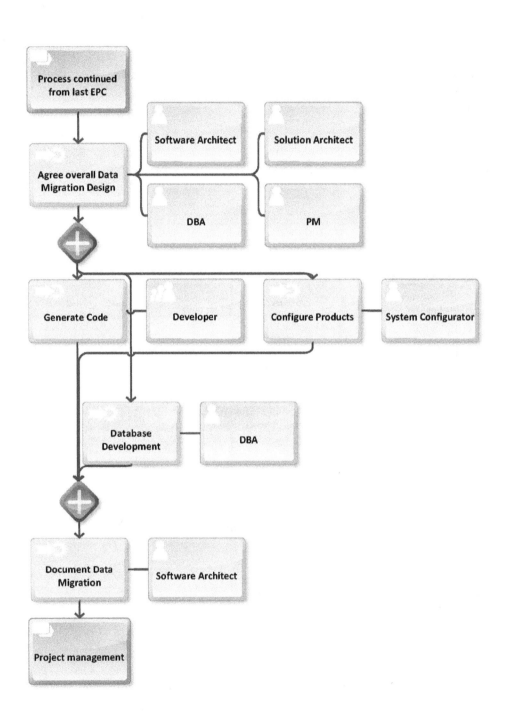

4.3.2.3.11 Conduct governance

Finally it is important to conduct governance. However governance is not just a something where an architect can feel important, but it is a well defined process to ensure maturity and lower risk.

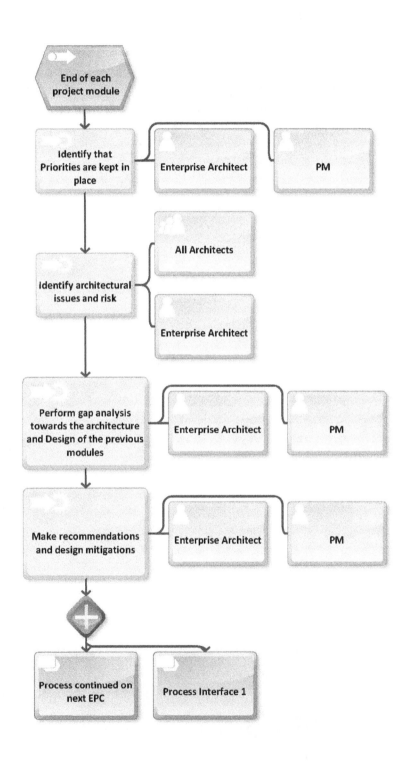

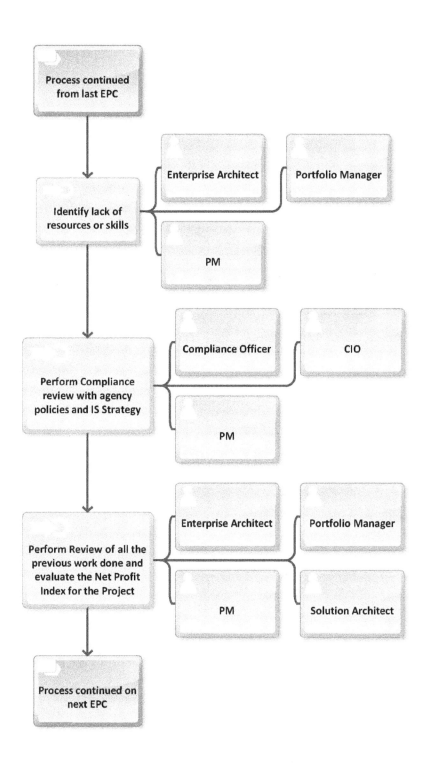

Process continued from last EPC

Identify lack of resources or skills

Enterprise Architect

Portfolio Manager

PM

Perform Compliance review with agency policies and IS Strategy

Compliance Officer

CIO

PM

Perform Review of all the previous work done and evaluate the Net Profit Index for the Project

Enterprise Architect

Portfolio Manager

PM

Solution Architect

Process continued on next EPC

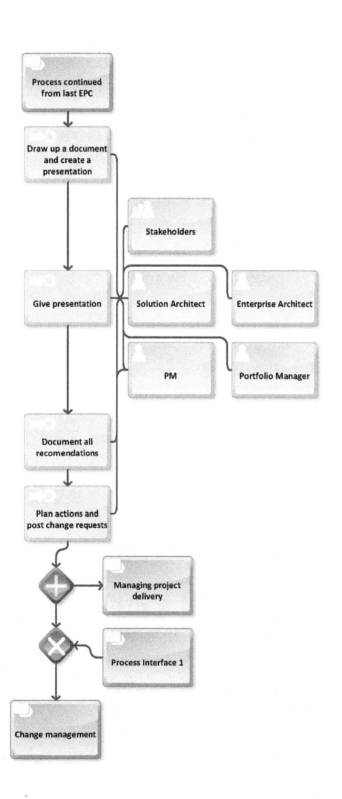

4.3.2.4 Technology architecture

After concluding the data and solution architecture the process will now move into the technology or Infrastructure Architecture. This process is built on a similar format than the last one as at the end of the day both architecture processes are handling technology.

4.3.2.4.1 Identify all technical services required

Here we will look at the services in Level 3 to 6 as defined in chapter 3 and plan them into services.

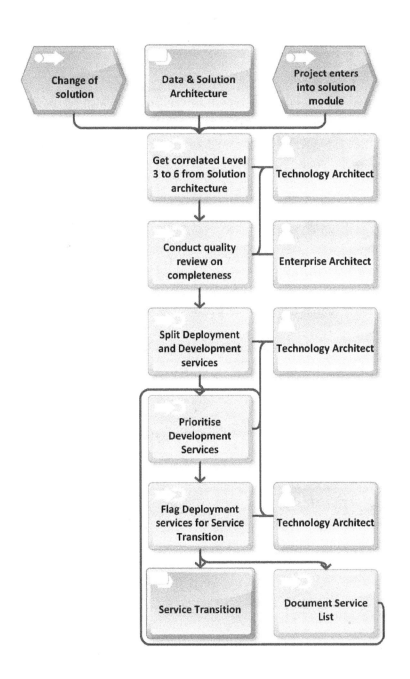

Change of solution

Data & Solution Architecture

Project enters into solution module

Get correlated Level 3 to 6 from Solution architecture

Technology Architect

Conduct quality review on completeness

Enterprise Architect

Split Deployment and Development services

Technology Architect

Prioritise Development Services

Flag Deployment services for Service Transition

Technology Architect

Service Transition

Document Service List

4.3.2.4.2 Create overall technical architecture

This is the core process in the infrastructure architecture where the real architectural work is described, with checks on reuse, integration in SLM and the creation of the interaction of all the service for the project.

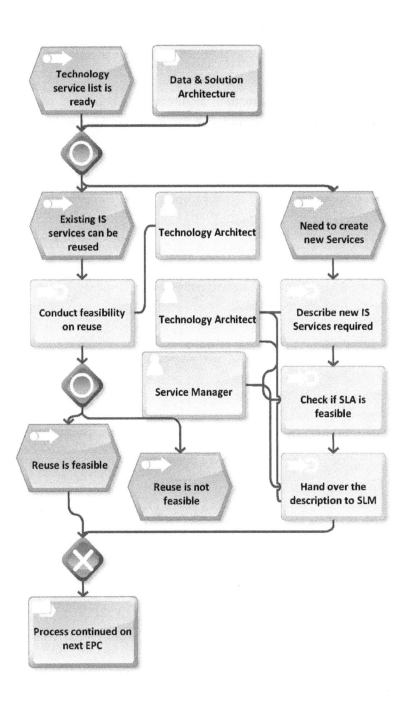

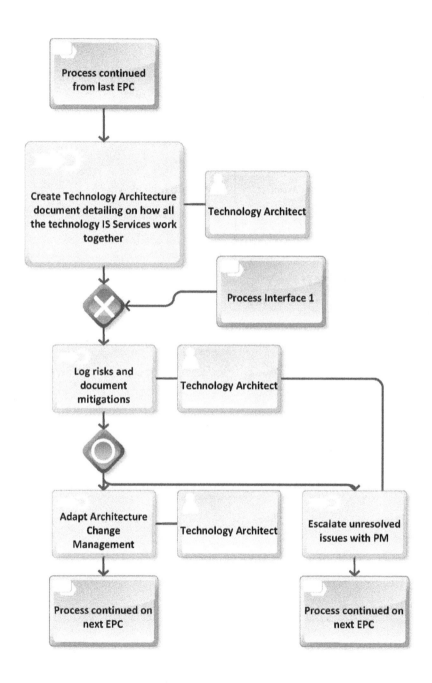

Process continued
from last EPC

Create Technology Architecture
document detailing on how all
the technology IS Services work
together

Technology Architect

Process Interface 1

Log risks and
document
mitigations

Technology Architect

Adapt Architecture
Change
Management

Technology Architect

Escalate unresolved
issues with PM

Process continued on
next EPC

Process continued on
next EPC

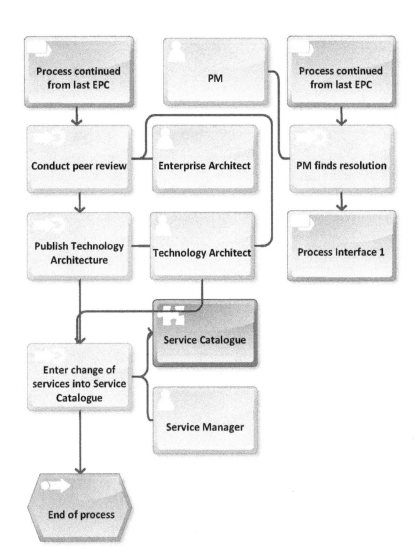

4.3.2.4.3 Create technical architecture on work packages

Technical or infrastructure architecture in a non service based process was often delivered as one package and this often made reuse a bit hard. Once we design everything in services we still have the problem that certain infrastructure components are best designed in work packages that consist out of many services that are delivered by one supplier. This kind work packaging that will ensure a maximum on ease of management with a minimum on dependencies will help the project to deliver faster.

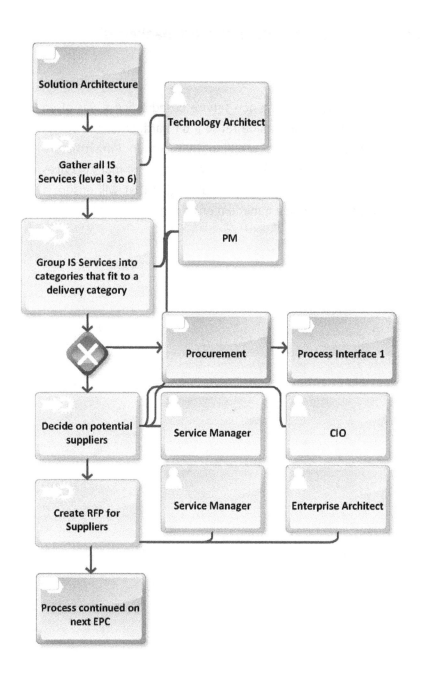

Solution Architecture

Technology Architect

Gather all IS Services (level 3 to 6)

Group IS Services into categories that fit to a delivery category

PM

Procurement

Process Interface 1

Decide on potential suppliers

Service Manager

CIO

Create RFP for Suppliers

Service Manager

Enterprise Architect

Process continued on next EPC

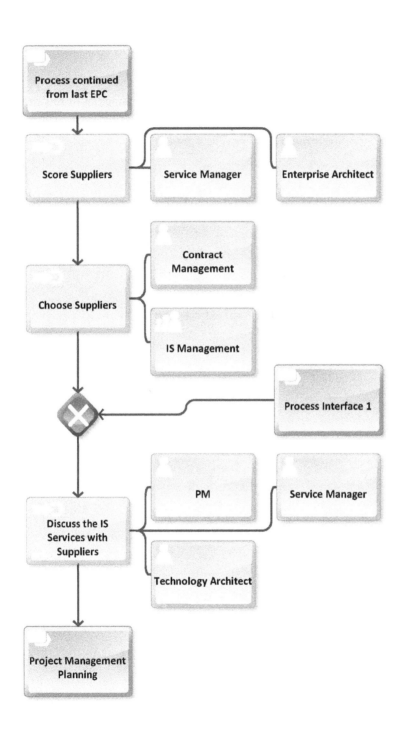

4.3.2.4.4 Integrate SLM into technical architectures

Before starting the designs the integration with Service Level Management has to be undertaken in a very similar approach as in the data and solution architecture.

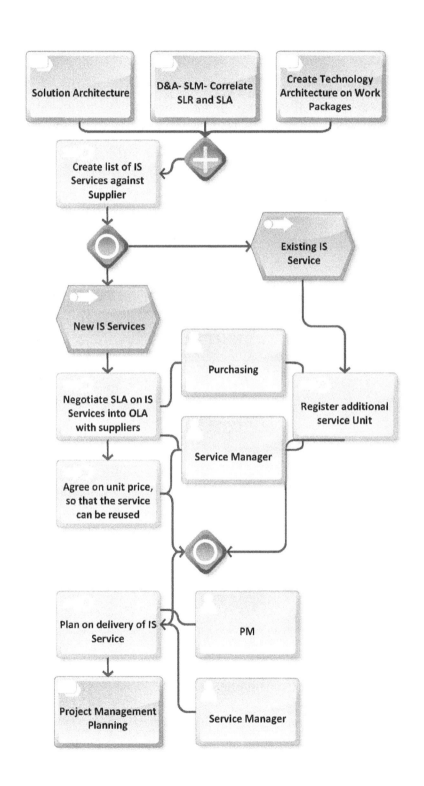

4.3.2.4.5 Create designs

The creation of the design in the infrastructure architecture will focus on the set-up of the environments, such as OS, networks as well the configuration of the directories within the parameter of the service levels.

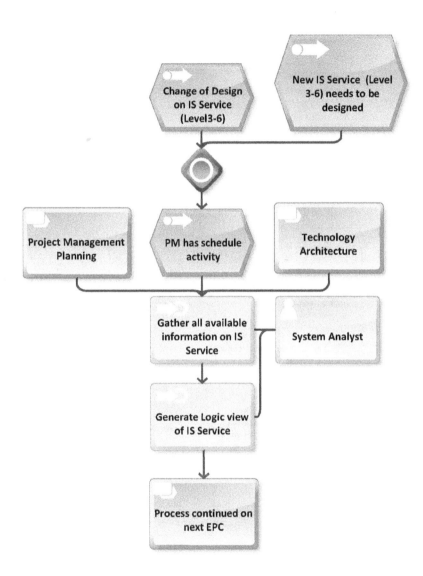

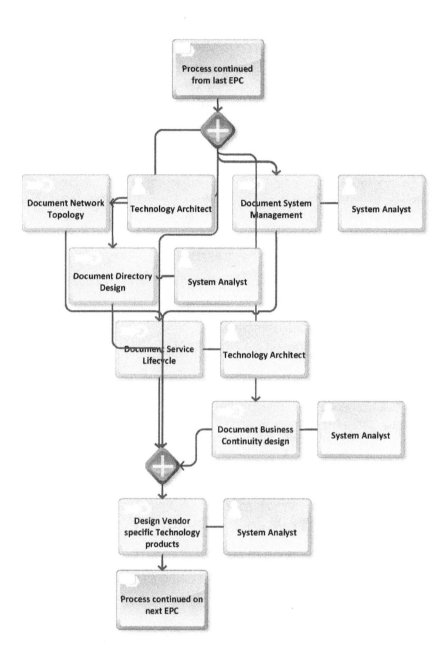

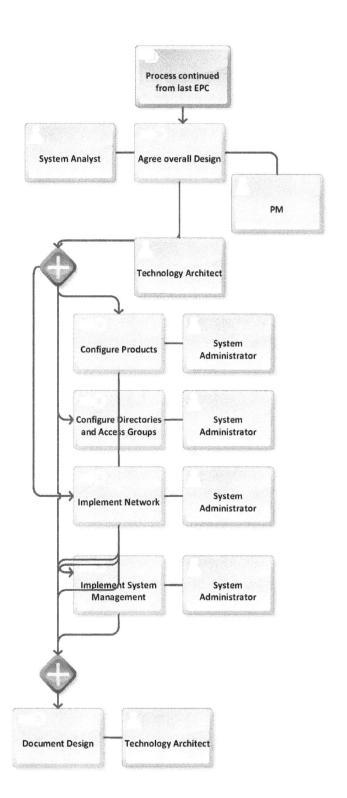

Process continued
from last EPC

System Analyst   Agree overall Design

PM

Technology Architect

Configure Products   System
Administrator

Configure Directories   System
and Access Groups   Administrator

Implement Network   System
Administrator

Implement System   System
Management   Administrator

Document Design   Technology Architect

4.3.2.4.6 Create test plans and test scripts

The creation of the test plans for the systems test is dependant on the conclusion of the technology architecture as the tests will be specified not only of the SLR and the business architecture, but also on the design decisions such the network topology and the specifics in implementing the SLR such as log shifting or specific cluster designs.

When talking about the system test it is important to understand what the system tests entail:

- ✓ Scalability & Reliability Tests

- ✓ GUI, Usability & Compliance Tests

- ✓ Load & Stress Tests

- ✓ Error Handling, Maintenance and Installation Tests

- ✓ Recovery & Fail over Tests

- ✓ Preliminary security Tests

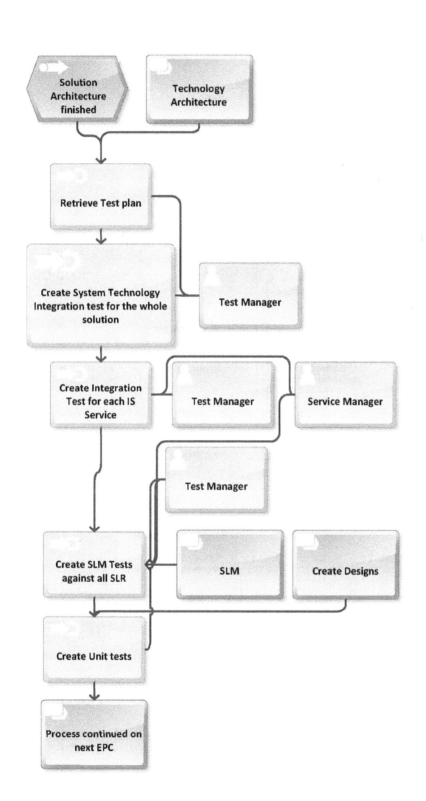

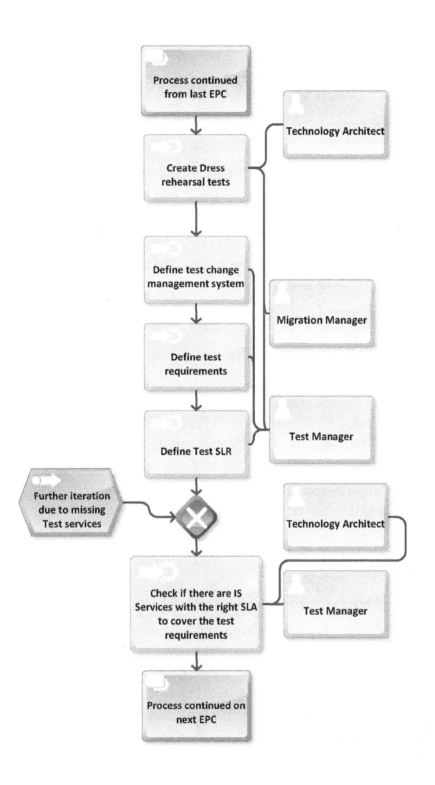

Process continued from last EPC

Create Dress rehearsal tests

Technology Architect

Define test change management system

Migration Manager

Define test requirements

Define Test SLR

Test Manager

Further iteration due to missing Test services

Technology Architect

Check if there are IS Services with the right SLA to cover the test requirements

Test Manager

Process continued on next EPC

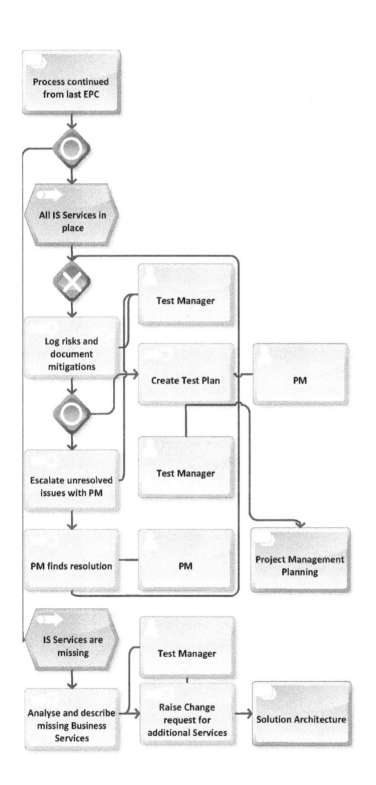

Process continued
from last EPC

All IS Services in
place

Test Manager

Log risks and
document
mitigations

Create Test Plan

PM

Escalate unresolved
issues with PM

Test Manager

PM finds resolution

PM

Project Management
Planning

IS Services are
missing

Test Manager

Analyse and describe
missing Business
Services

Raise Change
request for
additional Services

Solution Architecture

4.3.2.4.7 Identify opportunities

Identifying opportunities on technology architecture is mandatory as all services in this area need to be reusable and put to multiple uses.

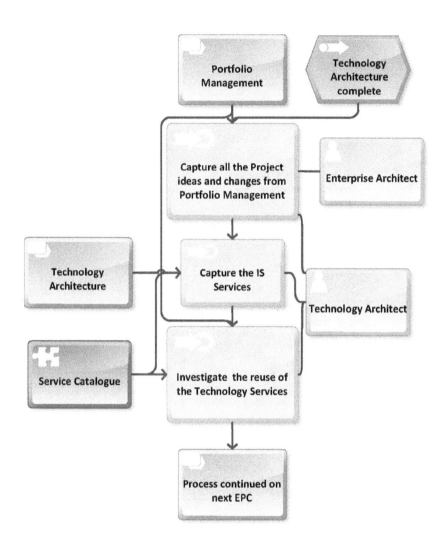

Portfolio Management

Technology Architecture complete

Capture all the Project ideas and changes from Portfolio Management

Enterprise Architect

Technology Architecture

Capture the IS Services

Technology Architect

Service Catalogue

Investigate the reuse of the Technology Services

Process continued on next EPC

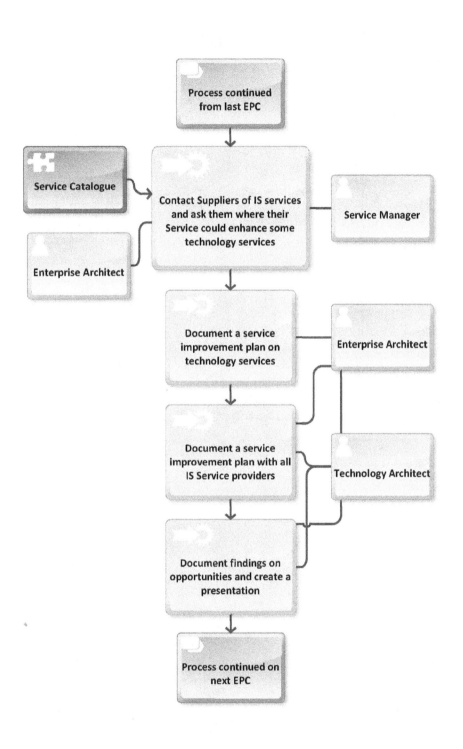

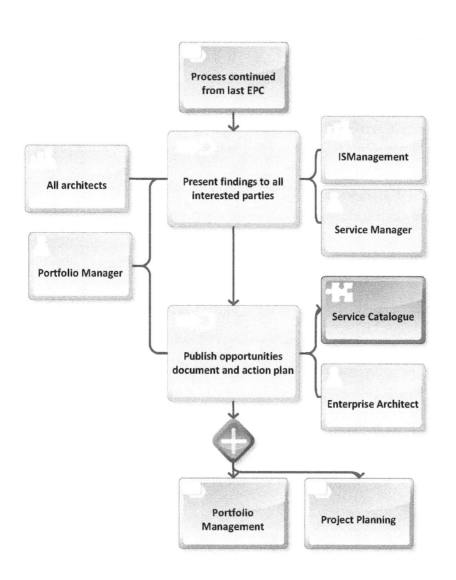

4.3.2.4.8 Design migrations

Migrations may be very important on infrastructure architect such as for upgrades where whole directory entries will need to be change on the day of going live and often cannot be tested before (e.g. migration of an IP address).

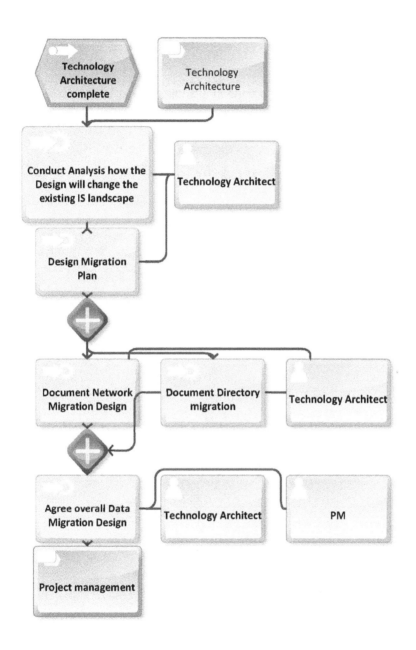

Technology Architecture complete

Technology Architecture

Conduct Analysis how the Design will change the existing IS landscape

Technology Architect

Design Migration Plan

Document Network Migration Design

Document Directory migration

Technology Architect

Agree overall Data Migration Design

Technology Architect

PM

Project management

4.3.2.4.9 Conduct governance

Governing the technology architecture is done in a similar way as in the data and solution architecture process.

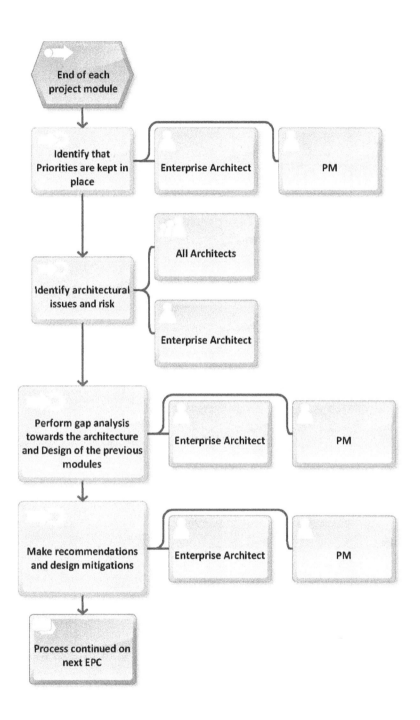

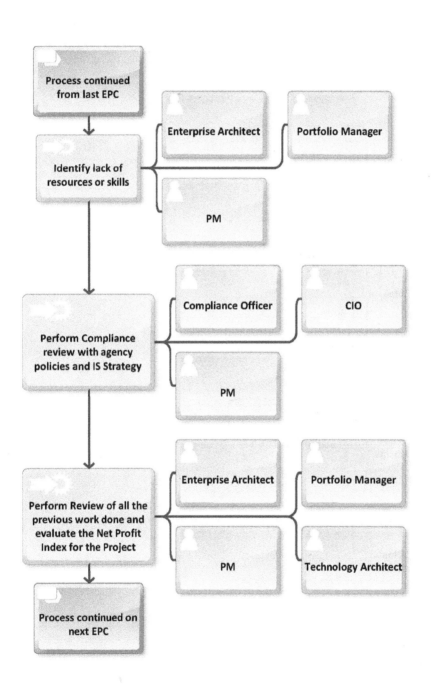

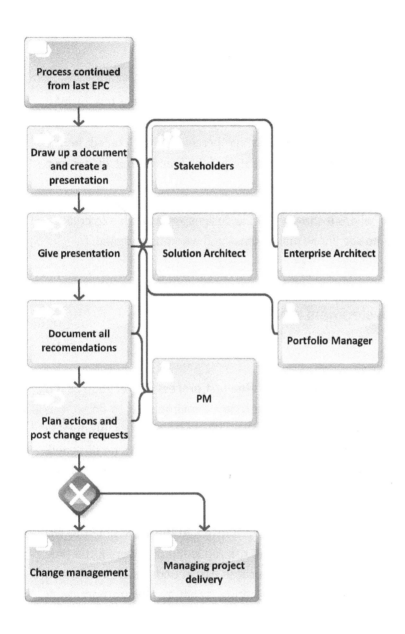

Process continued from last EPC

Draw up a document and create a presentation

Stakeholders

Give presentation

Solution Architect

Enterprise Architect

Document all recomendations

Portfolio Manager

Plan actions and post change requests

PM

Change management

Managing project delivery

4.3.2.5 Execution

The execution of the design & architecture processes is ultimately one of least explored areas of any IS frameworks, so instead of being able to find the ideal thread out of many good books and existing processes as detailed in the introduction to chapter 4 I had often to create a best practise out of my own experience.

Execution is the process where it shows if all the designs are workable to create a solution. Testing is then to see if it all makes sense and works as designed.

4.3.2.5.1 Create development environments

The creation of development environments is the first process in execution as it is not possible to develop a solution before there is an environment to do so. It is important that this environment will assemble the tests and the production environments very closely. To do this all environments have first to be designed. There is a tendency in pre-process IS led projects first to get a development environment together as soon as possible so that the code can be written. However that in term then often creates the situation where the architecture and the design are done as a token after the code is written. At the same time this will also kill any enterprise architecture on reuse, risk reduction or lowering the time to market. Usually this is then called agile because that sounds much better than non organised or ad-hoc development. The notion is that a software framework will do everything; which is proven to be wrong within the last 30+ years. Relying on software frameworks is such easy way that will avoid people from follow a process that it is normally still done because of convenience.

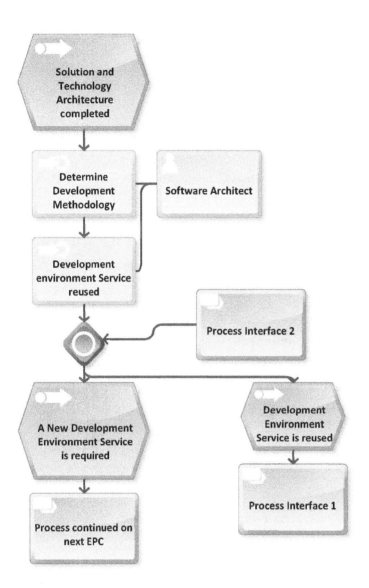

Solution and Technology Architecture completed

Determine Development Methodology

Software Architect

Development environment Service reused

Process Interface 2

A New Development Environment Service is required

Development Environment Service is reused

Process continued on next EPC

Process Interface 1

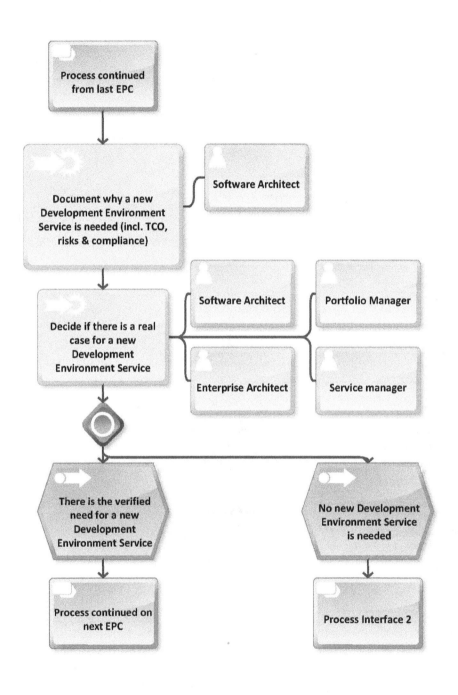

Process continued
from last EPC

Document why a new
Development Environment
Service is needed (incl. TCO,
risks & compliance)

Software Architect

Decide if there is a real
case for a new
Development
Environment Service

Software Architect

Portfolio Manager

Enterprise Architect

Service manager

There is the verified
need for a new
Development
Environment Service

No new Development
Environment Service
is needed

Process continued on
next EPC

Process Interface 2

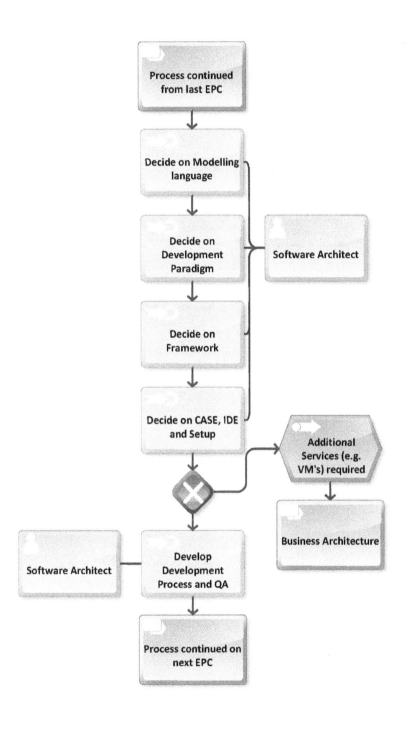

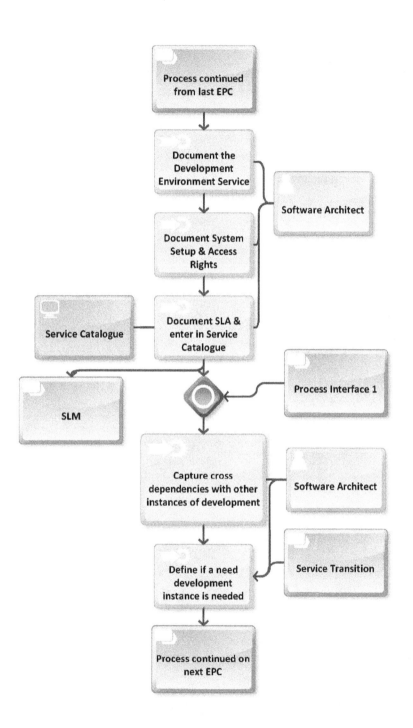

Process continued from last EPC

Document the Development Environment Service

Software Architect

Document System Setup & Access Rights

Service Catalogue

Document SLA & enter in Service Catalogue

SLM

Process Interface 1

Capture cross dependencies with other instances of development

Software Architect

Define if a need development instance is needed

Service Transition

Process continued on next EPC

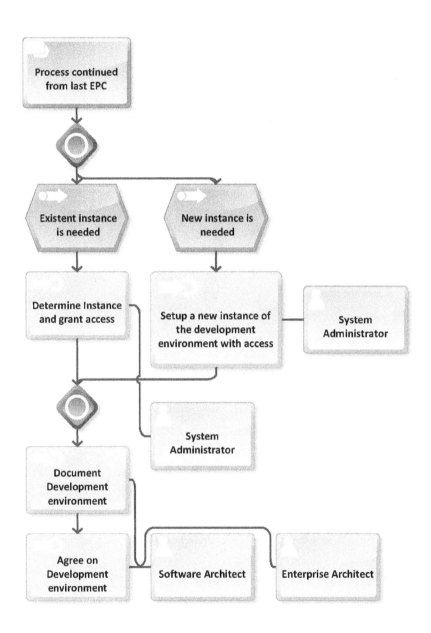

4.3.2.5.2 Develop solution

It might be strange to find the development process so late in the overall process; however the development can first start once the design is finished and the development environment is in place. If the design was done properly in terms of describing all the required developments in detail this should not be a problem.

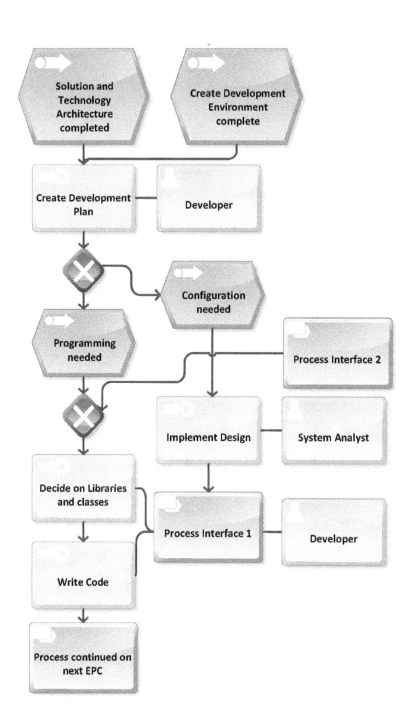

Solution and Technology Architecture completed

Create Development Environment complete

Create Development Plan — Developer

Configuration needed

Programming needed

Process Interface 2

Implement Design — System Analyst

Decide on Libraries and classes

Process Interface 1 — Developer

Write Code

Process continued on next EPC

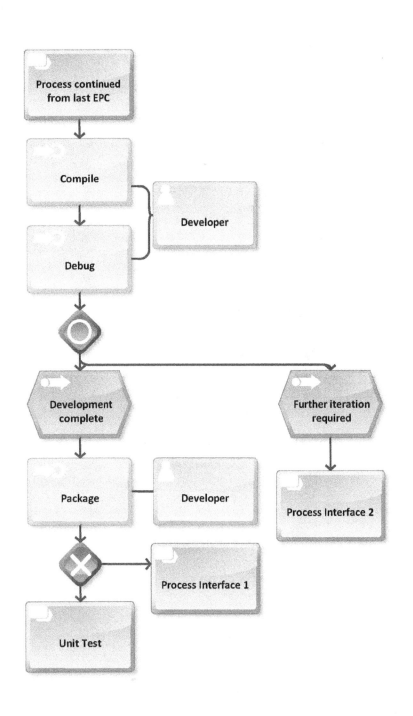

4.3.2.5.3 Deploy solution

Instead of the execution the process is often also called deployment, as most of the work involved is really about deployment. When deploying a solution it is important to do this in conjunction with the release management in service transition as the deployment defines the point where the service is transitioned into the service operation.

So from this point onwards the management of the design & architecture process is no longer exclusively done by the project manager, but shared with the service transition management.

It should also be noted that it sometimes becomes necessary to update a service during this process so again it is important to update the release management for the specific service.

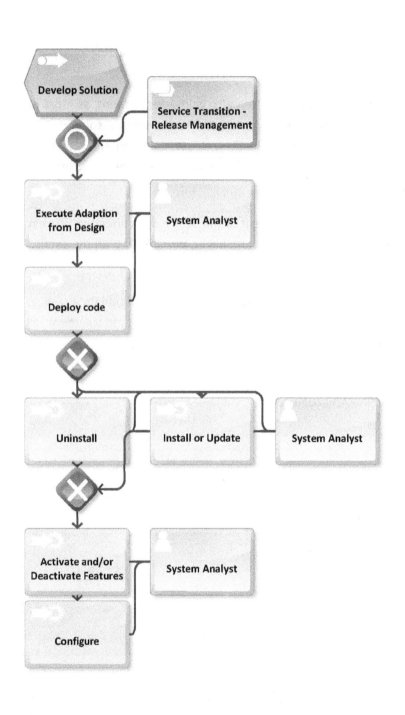

4.3.2.5.4 Create test environments

After the successful deployment process the creation of a test environment is a very simple process.

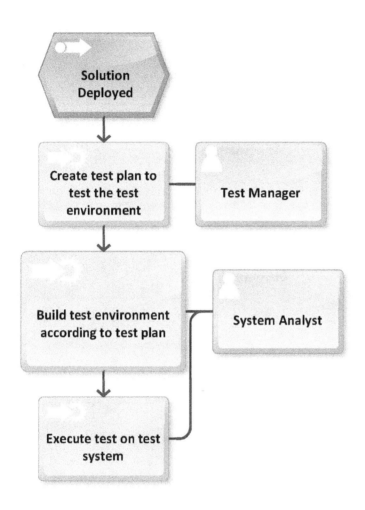

4.3.2.5.5 Create live environments

The creation of the production environment include two tests that are performed in the test environment as well, but which need to be rerun on the live environment as only the live environment will have the full specification of hardware and the live security settings.

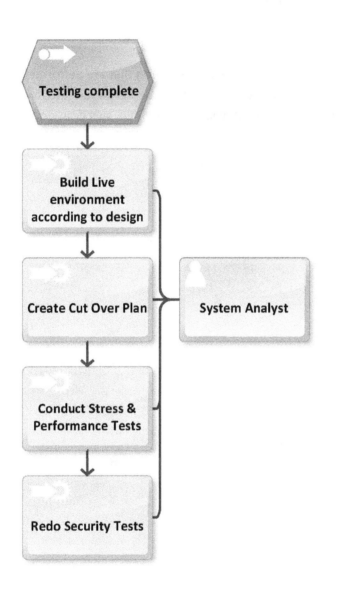

Testing complete

Build Live environment according to design

Create Cut Over Plan

Conduct Stress & Performance Tests

Redo Security Tests

System Analyst

4.3.2.5.6 Conduct dress rehearsals

Once all tests are finished many enterprises will deploy a solution without a second taught, just to discover that some parts went wrong in the same way as performing a live play and just testing all things in isolation of each other. This is why the dress rehearsal in IS projects is of the utmost importance as it will at least give you a smooth going live and as they say, first impression count.

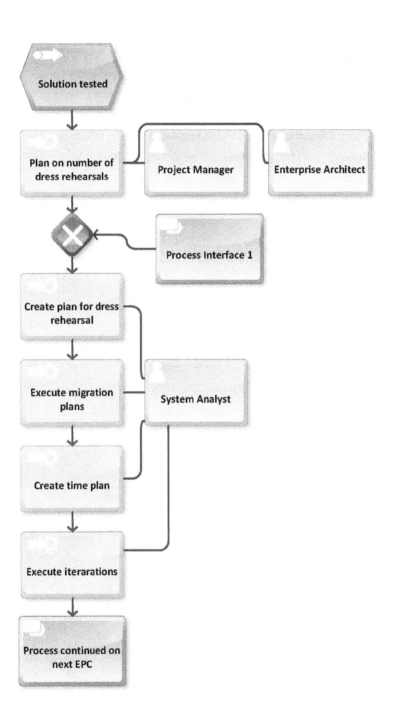

Solution tested

Plan on number of dress rehearsals

Project Manager

Enterprise Architect

Process Interface 1

Create plan for dress rehearsal

Execute migration plans

System Analyst

Create time plan

Execute iterarations

Process continued on next EPC

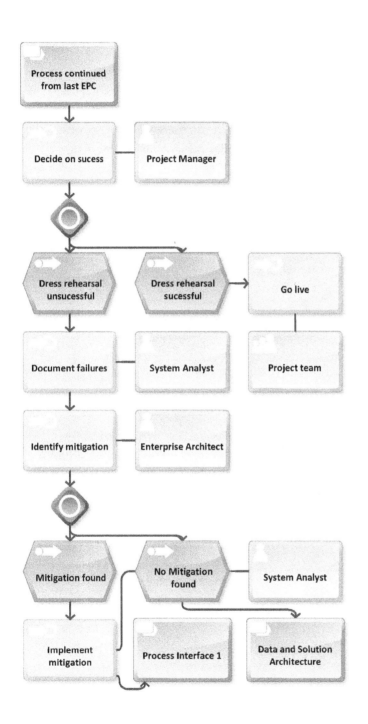

Process continued from last EPC

Decide on sucess — Project Manager

Dress rehearsal unsucessful

Dress rehearsal sucessful → Go live

Document failures — System Analyst

Project team

Identify mitigation — Enterprise Architect

Mitigation found

No Mitigation found — System Analyst

Implement mitigation

Process Interface 1

Data and Solution Architecture

4.3.2.6 Testing

Testing is the last level 2 process in design & architecture. Testing as a process is one of the oldest and best established processes in some areas, however often it is described in models such as the famous V model rather than a logical step by step process that is required to gain real maturity.

Within the test processes I will mostly just present the process in terms of the flow rather than to rewrite or copy paste material easily found elsewhere, as I want to see this book mainly filling the gaps instead of just reheating existing output via the famous copy & paste method.

4.3.2.6.1 Conduct unit tests

Unit testing could also be presented together with the development as it done by the same developers that have just written the code. The only very important thing in unit tests is to only test the unit (often classes) without all the other code around (isolation).

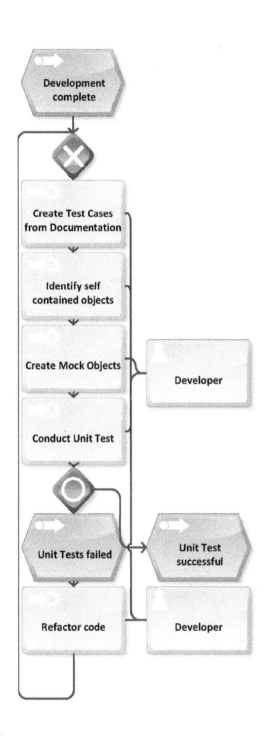

4.3.2.6.2 Conduct integration tests

The integration test is the first one that is performed and managed by the testing team and that contains the additional loop to decide if a test fails if this can be fixed or if there is design flaw.

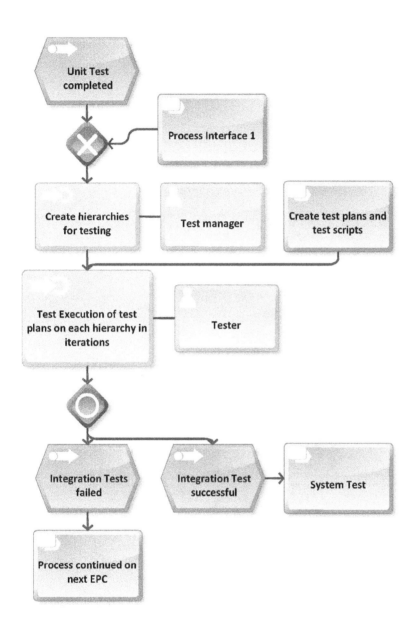

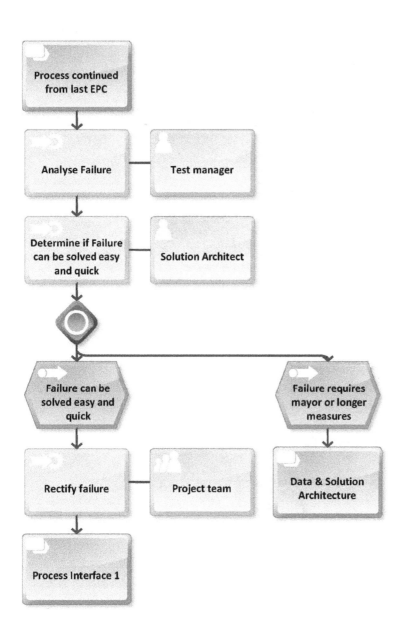

4.3.2.6.3 Conduct systems tests

For system tests is sometimes a very good idea to share the results with the whole team, even those not involved directly as it is good place for learning.

The elements of the system tests are described in chapter 4.3.2.4.6.

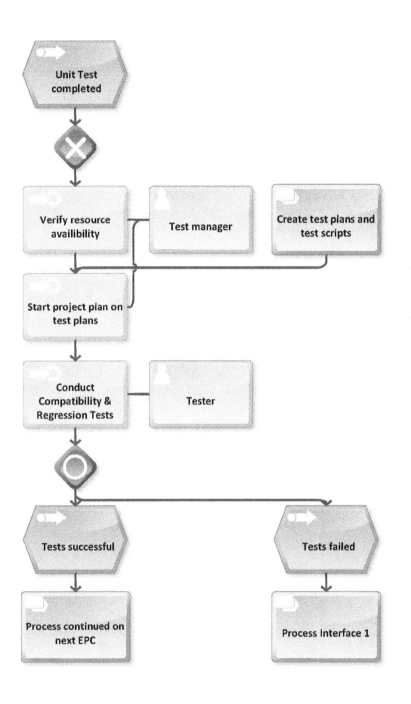

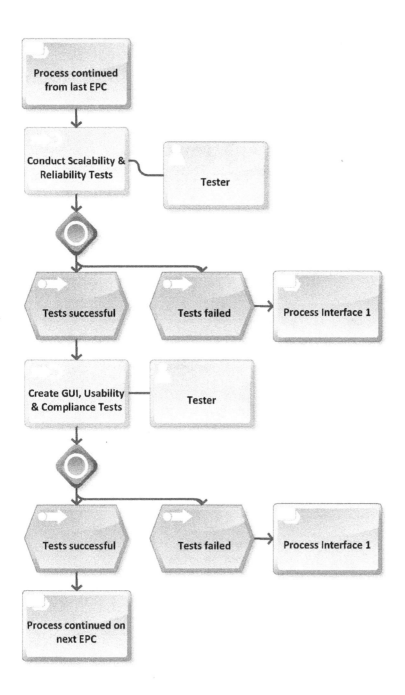

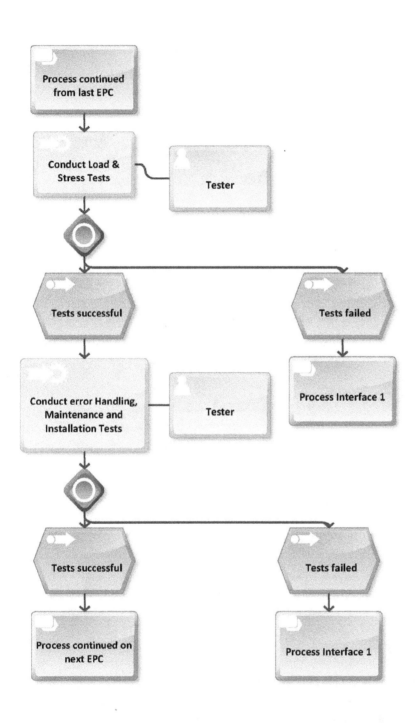

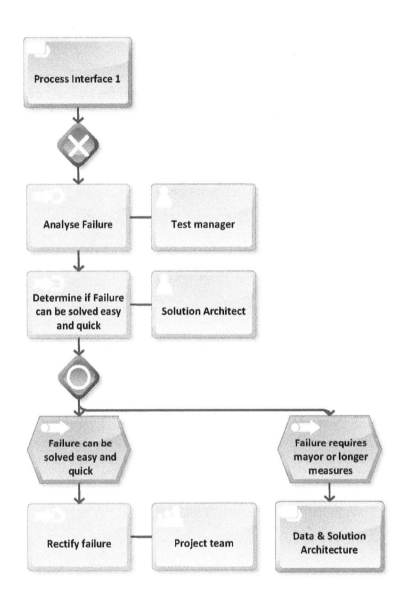

4.3.2.6.4 Conduct User Acceptance Tests

The user acceptance test is the most important test as this tests what the business owner was expecting. It is just important to plan the date well ahead to ensure that the key users are available.

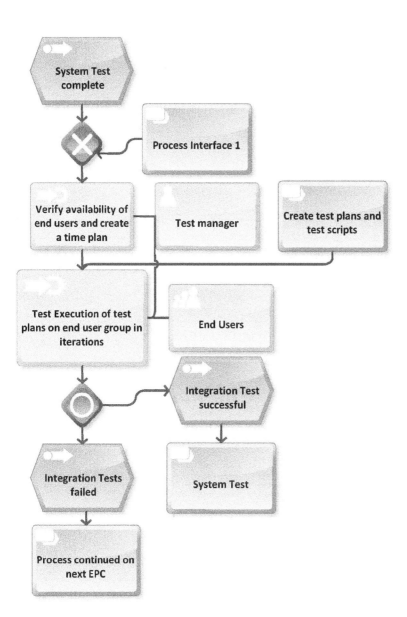

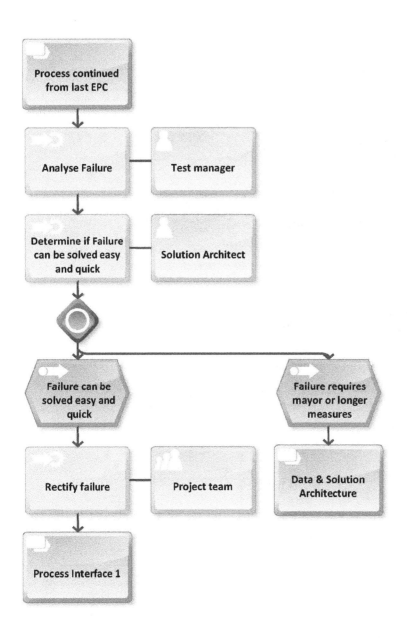

4.3.2.6.5 Conduct SLM Tests

This process to test the validity of the SLA is often forgotten, but very important for the successful service transition.

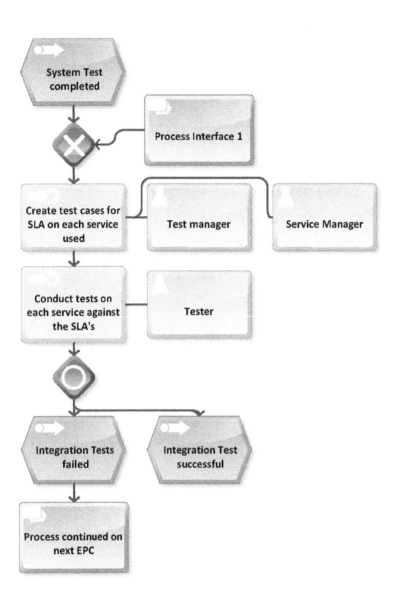

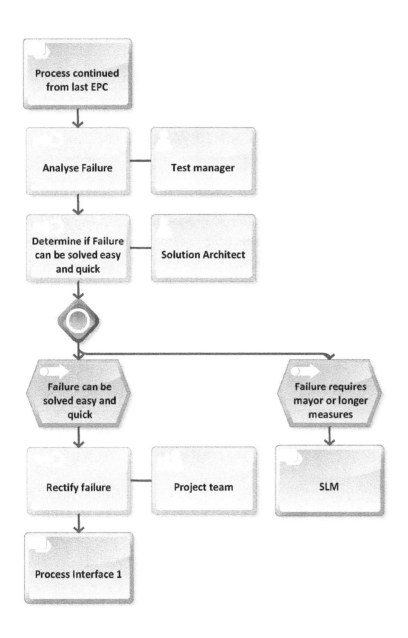

4.4 Value Check

By implementing a best practise on architecture within any enterprise there is usually one distraction happening, which has to do with the documentation and the way it is written. There is always a big move towards standard artefacts and a great discussion on them often followed by another wave on tools and completely empty of ROI or process. If the enterprise architect can manage to steer away from the artefact discussion and only concentrate on the two tools mentioned in the processes the ROI with the cost spent within every project will drop by approximately 30 % once the process enters the maturity level of CMMI level 3. If the enterprise architect can not stop the standard documentation discussion on the worst level the result will be a negative ROI.

The plain fact is that IS processes will create financial benefits, whereas standard artefacts maybe nice and wile the discussions are good for the intellect, they do not translate into financial or speed to market benefits. The other area of savings is in project management as it is always easier and quicker (time to market) to manage a given process.

Implementing a standard way of operation in architecture will also ensure a much lower risk as it is much more likely that nothing is forgotten in the process.

5. Use of standard business processes

Always drink upstream from the herd.

Will Rogers

5.1. Value

By using standard business processes rather than bespoke ones it is possible to use preconfigured systems and to ensure that the mistakes in process design that have been eliminated through many years of process improvement are not repeated. As such there is a large cost improvement with much less investments

The risks are lowered as the standard business processes are optimised for the lowest risk profile through many decades of refinements.

The use of standard ready made business processes clearly improves the time to market over customised business processes.

5.2 Introduction

In 2009 M Kohlbacher presented an empirical study showing that enterprises using Business Process Management gain higher customer satisfaction, product quality, delivery speed and time-to-market speed (The Effects of Process Orientation on Customer Satisfaction, Product Quality and Time-Based Performance. Paper presented at the 29th International Conference of the Strategic Management Society, Washington DC, October 11–14).

There is usually just one twist to the story that most companies still use custom designed processes apart from some standard processes on which this specific study is build. The few commonly known business processes that have already gained such a large influence are the R2R (Record to Report), P2P (Plan to Produce) and S2P (Source to Pay) that is often also named Procure to Pay.

Attached find a complete list of all the business processes in Appendix B that are used in most industries; additionally there are some common business processes in each mayor industry (also defining education as an industry, so industry is not defined as a commercial set-up). Those specific industry processes I am not including in this book, but I am discussing them in my Netcast. The IS business processes described in the previous chapter are of course not part of this list.

All these processes are always using a top level BPM level (e.g. Order-To-Cash), several 2nd level processes (e.g. Shipment) and then several 3 level processes containing each a distinct set of activities (e.g. Freight Management).

The list presented in this book is not conclusive and does not have any guarantee on completeness, but is merely a collection of BPM work conducted by myself in the past. Almost all of the business processes in the Appendix are supported by many ERP vendors.

The list deliberately does not contain business processes that are vendor specific. While there are many vendor specific business process description it is hard to find a vendor neutral reference site, despite many attempts in locating it.

For enterprise architecture it is however only important to know of the content of a business process to the extend that is might be reused in another area or to stop enterprises designing customised processes where there is a standard process in place. Another added requirement on behalf of the enterprise architect is to know on specifics on implementing the process in a manner done across the industry, as to use a standard business process, but then create a bespoke system for it or to use the wrong kind of system.

A small site caution needs to be given to enterprise architects not to apply their usual first choice of technologies in all areas. An example of this is the standard process in procurement to ascertain purchasing lists via the very primitive method of punch-out; a technology based on screen scraping a web page of a supplier. Instead most enterprise architects will prefer a nice web service, as this is neater, however since the procurement industry is using punch-out as a very cheap, low operation costs for years any decision on technology changes against the standard business model always needs to checked against the value based approach unless your enterprise is based on a different motivational model discussed in chapter 2.

5.3. The detailed enterprise architecture process

Within the standard industry process section I will give a short explanation on each process with some observations in all different areas of architecture. As a health warning this is mainly based on my own experience and therefore biased towards mainly European issues. Also all these notes will just highlight some of issues from my experience, so I hope that at a later version this chapter will be expanded.

The chapter will only focus on the cross industry processes and even there on some hand-picked once as I am self publishing the book and it will otherwise get too expensive if I exceed a certain number of pages.

This chapter is however not describing standard IS business services and application services for each process as this would require another full book.

5.3.1 The "Hire-to-Retire" (H2R) process

This level 1 process that is often refereed to as the Hire-to-Fire process is one of the processes that require a highly skilled enterprise architect as it is both complex and always attached to a lot legal and compliance work.

When attempting to tackle this process most enterprise architects will do one mistake out of two. Either they will trust the ERP vendor completely or they want to understand everything in detail. Trusting vendors may sometimes work depending on the quality of their consultants, but it is important to ask them the right questions, which this chapter is there for. On the other side trying to capture all requirements in detail is a task in this process that will result in never going forward as there are usually weekly changes in terms of a specific law or best practices.

In the eighties and in the nineties the H2R process was divided into Personnel Administration and Personnel Development (PA & PD). This was done for two very compelling reasons. The first centred on the idea that PA should be done either by a computer or by low paid clerks, where PD was an area for skilled professionals (also known as Human Resource Managers) that would help the executive management with career progression.

The second and today still predominant area was that PA was managed by Finance, since the main output is the payroll which is part of Account Payable (AP) and should therefore be in the domain of Finance, while PD was given to its own Department called HR or HCM (Human Capital Management).

However if this idea is extended you could classify sales as part of the Account Receivable (AR) and Purchasing as AP. This is the main reason why PA and PD where merged to H2R process. Another important factor is of course that this process merger also eliminated many interfaces.

Security is one of the main concerns in any HR or HCM system as under most legislation the data is highly confidential, as it is possible to do identity theft with this data.

Now security analysts have developed an interesting rule set that is accepted in most jurisdictions. This rule set or best practise expresses that the highest data classification in any IT system will dictate the overall security settings. In practise this is causing a lot of problems and often leads to a separation of the HCM systems from other ERP or enterprise systems.

There are also many other concerns in such systems, especially in the public sector were it can happen that the personnel files of special agents or just private addresses of police officers can lead to much harm. So HCM systems for police forces for example need special scrutiny.

The H2R process therefore will need to be implemented with the notion that it requires constant updates into the personnel administration. This and the fact that the R2H process requires a higher data security level than other ERP like systems is also the reason why it recommended running this system in a separate ERP instance.

Another note of caution should be added at this juncture, implementing this process never adds any credit to the implementer; and implementing it just slightly wrong will give the architect a lot of grief as every staff member is affected.

5.3.1.1 Recruitment and selection

For recruitment and selection it is very important to remember to find a balance of a nice looking way of the e-Recruitment website together with the right amount of security. Any data that is entered into recruitment has to be handled with great care and should only be very selectively used in any open form of communications such as email. The classical example here is that after a candidate enters his interest an email with all his/her sensitive information is sent on his/her present company email.

5.3.1.1.1 Sourcing Resumes

Sourcing resumes is usually done in two ways either directs or via a dedicated website; advert in a news paper, etc. or through agencies. It is important to keep both of these data sources separate from each other, as candidates that go though an agent come with an added commission, while those via direct means will not require this add on.

Before starting with the sourcing per se the process needs to identify the salary range, possible bonuses and other benefits; additionally the job description should be prepared.

Here it is of some benefit if the system has templates for the hiring manager to use, so it is of great use to save the previous job descriptions as well as the entry passages. The job description should also always have a quantifiable part so that the new hire later can be measured on them.

It is also advisable to create a scoring with weighting at this time which will make the consequent screening much easier. Another useful feature is to define a minimum skill set to avoid coming up with too many candidates for screening.

Any source will require a field on identification to enable the consequent HR analytic.

Data from agents are transferred towards screening right a way while those entered the other way first need to be processed further. The first step is usually the sending of an acknowledgment. Here it is necessary to check on the national HR regulations how this will need to happen as some countries have very strict rules and even require an ID check to guarantee that the person in question really wants to apply.

The second part is then to conduct a pre-screening that will check if the application meets the requirements (e.g. copy of a health certificate for chefs) or if certain key words are included in the resume. This pre-screening is usually automated and sometimes leads to some funny misunderstandings (e.g. Candidate has no Java experience only J2EE).

For sourcing to work well a clear master data management of job offers need to be implemented as well as on candidates. This is very important if your enterprise uses agents, as a successful candidate clearly need to be identified to its source as for agency fees; another consideration is that many agencies have a clause in their contract that if your enterprise hires the candidate they submitted for another position in the next 6 month your enterprise will have to pay the full fee.

From an organisational process viewpoint there is the process of recruitment agencies that will try to cut this process of and start to pressure the hiring manager to choose from their selection. This may be possible when hiring contractors (such as the author) as this is just a purchase order, but on the staff hiring this will cause lots of problems. This said the sourcing process will also need to allow for retainers for adverts or for agencies, where an enterprise policy that apply against the standard hiring process can be dictated.

Sourcing resumes also has to be set up with financials in the AP.

5.3.1.1.2 Screening

Screening is the second process in hiring that will require a lot of process engineering if done right. Screening is a task that is always done in iterations, but where each iteration can be slightly different.

Usually there is always a non interview screening, followed by interviews. At any point it is important after each step to gather the results in an electronic form either to determine the next steps or to note down not to continue with a note on the reason so that the candidates will be informed. At the same time it is important that all notes are held in the system, especially if an interview process goes over 10 or more iterations where the last person may not get the picture any more otherwise. Another reason for keeping the record is in the fact that any weaknesses may be used in the consequent personnel development or used for a smaller entry salary.

In screening many companies also create assessment centres for a better skill selection or other reasons. So the screening process needs to support this kind of centres, a good work flow, a communications suite and the associated financials. Sometimes it may also be advisable to contact candidates that have not made it in person, specifically if they will stay in the same industry and may become customers in the future. So do not try to automate everything, just make sure that through automation no one falls through the cracks.

The screening process will of course always be allowed to be sidelined if the ideal candidate is already known before and the job opening was designed specifically for her/him.

5.3.1.1.3 Offer closure

Once the screening is over often there is a list of preferred hires and some backups should the candidates not want to accept the offerings. The systems always need to be able to compute this.

Another important part of this process is to determine the exact offer for each candidate as not every candidate will qualify on the same terms. The offer needs to include all bonuses and benefits and the start date.

The only main other large tasks that need to be performed here are reference checks and sometimes security checks. As these checks are performed by external agencies it is often useful to create standard secured interfaces to these agencies with integration to the purchasing system for billing.

This process is usually straight forward from here and will close with the positive response of a hire. However before the hire starts and has worked for some weeks or month the process data still need to be present, if the new hire for example turns out not to be as good as taught.

5.3.1.1.3 New hire integration

The new hire integration is a process that is more important than most people believe, as it will ensure that the new hire gets the first appreciation of the enterprise as well that it ensures that the new hire is starting to create value as soon as possible.

This process will not only be feed by the previous one, but also needs to be linked with the contractor (or temp) hire from purchasing.

One of the areas most impacted is IT as most new hires require a whole lot of IT credentials, hardware and software. At the same time facility management and corporate security are affected. It is therefore highly advisable to create automatic work flows to the departments and to the hiring manager, ideally in a two way communication so that the new hire can be sent a letter or mail containing the contact persons and a clear itinerary for his/her first day.

5.3.1.1.4 Compliance

Compliance is an important part of the process in hiring. It will monitor for example the compliance on gender, disability and ethnic considerations.

I just need to mention at this point if you construct the hiring process on a global scale on your enterprise this process and some other will be very different in each jurisdiction, as you might be obliged to ask certain questions on ethnics in one country and in another country this may be an offense. So here it always important to be very sensitive which part of the Hire-to-Retire process makes sense to be implemented globally and which parts should be restricted to one jurisdiction.

5.3.1.1.4 Self-Service

Self-Service in hiring mainly touches on e-Recruitment. Security is a good reason that enterprises will not allow to much of the hiring process as an unguided self service for managers.

E-Recruitment mainly focuses on the point that new hires will enter all their information via a security protected portal and help with the selection by self evaluation, saving valuable time on HR professionals.

However here it is always important to determine if potential good new hires will fill out the questionnaire or only the unemployable ones. A very good integration into E-Recruitment is for example the check on the minimum qualifications, such as specific certifications with numbers that can be checked. Again for some areas interfaces to reference systems might be of great use here.

5.3.1.2 Training and development

Training and Development is a process that is mostly budget driven. This is very important as many staff will always think that it is need driven. Training and development builds on hierarchy of needs and then is delivered by training partners.

Here it is important to channel as many courses through a few providers as possible to get the most efficient value out of the process. This in itself is also the reason why many suggestions by staff are ignored. So when setting up this process as an enterprise architect in your company you have to take the consideration of the enterprise into higher degree than your own experience.

5.3.1.2.1 Needs analysis

The need for Training and development in an enterprise is driven by two hierarchies of need.

The first and more important is on the ability of the company to deliver its products and services. Here for example if your company produces oil pipelines it is most important that your technical blue collar workers get their certifications or re- certifications in welding , material examination and safety.

Training for a network administrator in IT will of course be of much less importance here, as the enterprise can still function without this.

The second hierarchy of need is driven by the retention of staff. As most staff is under the impression that training will always lift their market worth (in my view only partial true) it is important to establish a hierarchy of need here. However if as an enterprise your budget on training and development is very tight only the first hierarchy is used.

The best way to implement this is via a mangers self service, where each manager is given a certain number of points depending on number of staff so that she/he can not give a blanket high number on each staff.

The Training and Development needs will then be handed over to the purchasing department which then will try to purchase as much training and development as possible against the budget based on the hierarchies.

5.3.1.2.2 Administration

The administration of Training and Development mainly centres around the capture of training taken, especially the mandatory one and development given internally often in form of mentoring and trainings on the job.

The second part on training is the capture of all the certificates and uploading them against the personnel file. Since the training records often have direct impact on operations this need to be handled as a priority.

It should be considered to build standard interfaces to the largest training providers to automate this process. However it is important to add a note of caution on all interfaces with the Hire-to-Retire process that interfaces always contain sensible information and should always be encrypted and only decrypted at the HR systems themselves (end to end encryption) and not opened and re-encrypted at a message broker or ESB.

5.3.1.2.3 Material creation

Often it is important to create materials for Training and Development within an enterprise. This is often the case if IT is implementing a new system.

At the creation of all materials the reuse aspect and risk reduction needs to be considered so when creating the material the material needs to be produced in a way that it can be reused as a help and support function to refresh.

Often training materials are just stored on a file server and forgotten and later someone will have to re-write the same material for support. So this is why all materials should be stored and catalogued in a document management solution with access right management.

For training and development materials it is also important, always to create the interactive training material in a simple easy way to apply format so that it can be rendered without special software.

5.3.1.3 Benefits administration

Apart from the compensation management this process is one of the deal-breakers when you are judged against the implementation of a new HR system, as the benefits are often the reason that staff joins a specific enterprise.

Another important factor you should always keep in mind in benefits is that of the financial implications. Some benefits may be classified in some jurisdiction as payment in kind, so taxes will be deducted from the benefit amount, which in term make them less attractive. The other financial consideration is if benefits that require some contributions like pensions are paid from the gross or net salary, as this is very different in many countries and if the system would always take the most conservative approach throughout all countries you might deprive some colleagues of their pay (not a good career move).

5.3.1.3.1 Health & welfare

While the health & welfare process is very straight in some countries where the law almost dictates all parameters in this area, in other countries the whole subject is open from no mandatory benefits in this area towards a complete cover, so all my remarks may not always be coherent in this area.

The process often starts with the research in schemes offered with an annual enrolment offered to staff. Sometimes certain schemes are fixed to employment hierarchies or time within the enterprise. On the other hand in countries where the law is putting down the general guidelines this may just be an optional benefit or the staff may just inform the enterprise of his heath and welfare providers, while in other cases even that is fixed. So this is important to keep in mind on large global roll-outs.

Some countries in Europe even have such a bloated welfare system that the health and welfare insurers create more paperwork than any other part of the business combined. This of course also makes it expensive to employ staff, but once hired it is very hard to separate them from the enterprise.

Therefore it is most important that all of the health and welfare communications is done via interfaces to reduce the overhead. While in some countries the insurance providers will help with a standard interface in other countries where you can often even not chose the provider the interfacing gets very hard. For the enterprise architect it is therefore important to plan enough when attempting global roll outs and to source a system or service that can handle all these very different requirements against an otherwise very straightforward process mainly consisting of on e calculated AP per month per staff.

This process will also cover unemployment benefits, which are mandatory in certain countries and unheard in others.

5.3.1.3.2 Defined benefits

Both of the next processes are about pensions. The defined benefit pension is where the amount of pension is defined. This pension is often called final salary pension. So here the pension is defined as 100 % or another amount of the last pay or the average pay.

This kind of pension in many European countries is administrated and run by the government, while in most other areas of the globe it is run by the enterprise itself. In some countries it is also possible to have a combination of both in creating a basic defined benefit pension via the government and an added enterprise defined pension on top; often resulting with pensioners earning more than they ever did in employment.

Defined enterprise pensions have usually a variable contribution structure with the payment split between the company and the staff.

If you have this system within your enterprise you will then require an own pension system and invest the pensions wisely to create the funds required.

Additional the System or Service will have to post an quarterly or yearly report against the enterprise balance sheet informing if the pension plan is over or under performing since all under-performance will then be paid by the enterprise itself.

This has led many enterprises to close these schemes as the shortfall on the pension funds often has bankrupted otherwise healthy enterprises. However that often means that for some of the older workforce the schema is still in place and needs to be maintained.

5.3.1.3.3 Defined contributions

Defined contributions on the other hand mean that the employee will pay some amount in a fund and the enterprise will match his contribution. The match takes on different antilogarithms such as 1:1 or 1:1.5 and will then be paid in a selection of funds that the staff member decides on. This kind of pension in the US is often referred to as the 401 K. Administration of this kind of scheme if done properly in IS with interfaces to funds and internal interfaces and rules on maternity, paternity, illness, unpaid or paid leave, etc is pretty straight forward.

It should be noted that of course there is always the possibility for combining the defined contribution with the define benefit pension schemes.

5.3.1.3.4 Finance administrations

As mentioned in the introduction Finance is always the key part in the benefit administration as this process revolves around the AP. So all processes need to be audit proof and need to be embedded into finance down to the General Ledger.

This of course is especially true on the defined benefit pension as for the liability of the pension. So when implementing a Service or System for this a lot of reporting needs to be available as well as some predictions on liability.

5.3.1.3.5 ESS/MSS

Benefit administration creates a very large overhead, specifically in term of health insurance questions, exact pension numbers and approvals.

Enterprises will reduce this in two ways. The first way is constant information on the schemes and benefits. On the other hand all approvals and people management tasks are supported via a simple managers self service (MSS) always remembering that the manager in question will only access this system a couple of times each year.

Questions on health insurances and exact pension details should be provided to staff via an employee self portal to keep the overhead down.

5.3.1.4 Compensation management

Compensation management is certainly the most important process in the Hire-to-Retire process as it concerns everyone in the enterprise. There have been famous disasters in this area with some very good architects losing out for life. I actually know of some how were forced to migrate just to keep on working in their profession. My best recommendation is not to get distracted and follow through the complete architecture standard IS process described in chapter 4 of this book.

5.3.1.4.1 Payroll

Payroll is the oldest of all IS processes as it was the first process that got automated in the 5os and 60s. Payroll by its nature is also a classic batch process that is still done as a batch and should therefore it should always been insured that the processing power is in place.

Payroll itself is very different in industries and usually always requires more work in the blue collar segments than in the white collar area. Additional in countries that have a very regulated employment law and in enterprises that have a strong union lobby the rule of thumb is that the payroll grows more complicated, as the compensation is tried to be fair in all areas. This will then often consists of over 100 different overtime agreements and a very precise time recording.

Payroll also needs to take any holiday payments (in some countries by law the companies have to pay a bonus when someone is holiday), as well a 13th and even a 14th monthly salary into considerations.

In payroll it is also important to clearly document all deduction and added payments down to an almost self explanatory level, as upset with payroll data is the least desirable outcome.

The payroll will also need to ensure that the money is either paid on the right account or paid in cash with signature provided. This function needs to handled with great care as when people get divorced or other bad things are happening the pay is always of the highest concern.

The system should also allow to deduct certain amounts set by courts such as tax or paternity payments and make it impossible for the employee to change this.

Apart from these more traditional functions the payroll will also need to supply the Revenue Service with data and statistics. This often includes items such as benefits in kind (for example in the UK that is P11d form), the report on pay, the report on how many people got paid with disabilities (if there are not enough there is often a penalty) and many more. All these reports are required to be send at a certain date and always processed as batches.

5.3.1.4.2 Compensation review

Most companies conduct a compensation review once a year or even a longer period as it always is a drain on productivity. There are two main types of compensation review,.

The first one involves white collar workers with a higher salary that will have an individual review with their manager, where the manager is given a certain amount of compensation increase (sometimes decrease) and then will have to balance it on all the members of his department on a reward/need basis. This way requires a lot of detailed processing systems with a very clear audit trail. When department heads really want to get creative in this area, it often good to use a business rule system.

The second approach is that of a union agreeing a compensation review for al large part of the enterprise. However this kind of compensation review is very easy to implement.

5.3.1.4.3 Bonus plan administration

Bonus plans are paid in two very different ways and two different cycles. The traditional bonus is given on the whim of the boss (and him looking at the results) and then just added to the payroll at a given month (normally at the end of the financial year or quarter). This bonus system is still very much in existence in the banking industry.

The second kind of bonus is a direct link on sales figures and their billing or at reaching some levels of KPI's. Here the bonus plan administration system will need to be interfaced with the sales and finance systems and then the bonus is either paid on the next payroll or paid via AP.

5.3.1.4.4 ESS/MSS

Within compensation review there are many work flows required that can best be done via management self service. The main employee self service is nowadays the electronic payslip.

On the electronic payslip there are two things to note. The first is that you need to offer it as a download that is securely signed by your enterprise and offer a reference contact number as the payslips are often used to secure loans by the workforce.

The second main consideration is when your workforce is consisting of mainly low paid workers or you have a large sales force whose main income is on bonus you are likely to get an unpleasant peak behaviour in just the time that the payroll runs; so in the self service you need to cater for this peak while you still need the processing power for the payroll. This even happens on night-time as the fore said group needs to know down to the cent how much they can spent or when to pay a bill.

5.3.1.5 Performance management

Performance Management is one of the least loved processes and therefore should be automated as best as possible to ensure that the productive and staff motivation levels do not drop to much.

5.3.1.5.1 Performance review

Performance review should be set up well in advance in terms of the questions asked. This will ensure a smooth running and also make the process much fairer. So for this process it is important that there is system where the information is entered both from the manger as well as from the staff. Each question needs to be scored and then weighted in the background. The main question that needs special handling is on the improvements for the next period which needs to be inserted into the next review cycle.

Performance reviews systems also require a copy and paste function as many goals are identical to department goals and should as such be stored in a copy enabled template.

5.3.1.5.2 Progression management

Progression Management is a very important process that can also easily get out of hands. It is very important for HR professionals to plan a potential progression for the senior management and for key individuals so if they have an accident the enterprise can still function. It should be noted that if progression management is done for more than 20 % of the workforce the process is getting into an unsustainable TCO with the exception of known retirement or maternity.

This often happened in the early 90s when the process was first introduced in many enterprises and is still the reason that many executives will not want it to be implemented.

Progression management will always build on a potential date unless there is a clear date. This is why the system needs to be tuned on % of probability rather than on a fixed structure. Geographic consideration also will need to taken into consideration as well as data from the training system if a certification is required.

5.3.1.5.3 360 degree feedback

All feedback that involves your peers, your reports or your customers to report on should be offered in self service function. One of the main obstacles in this are is that people might not know how to fill these forms as they are not used to this. This is why a good help needs to provided and maybe even an assistance service in case of your customers.

5.3.1.5.4 ESS/MSS

Performance management is a process that should be done almost completely as an employee and manager self service with the exception of the core progression management part. But even there the input of the employee on a short list for progression should be gathered using the self service function.

5.3.1.6 Workforce management

Workforce management involves all the tasks that are traditional seen as those of HR visible to the wider enterprise, however almost all workforce management tasks are seen today as an ideal target for outsourcing. If these processes are outsourced please always remember that the data needs to be reported back into the enterprise.

5.3.1.6.1 Employee master data management

When contemplating on employee master data management without having worked on it most enterprise architects will think of a change in address, marriage, change of tax code, etc. that will not require a great deal of work in terms of IS. However there is a large complexity behind this which is called organisation management.

Within each enterprise there are two hierarchies in place, the most important for IT is the financial hierarchy that defines cost centres. However this hierarchy is often build on the organisational hierarchy defined in this process. The organisational hierarchy as the second hierarchy is also required for very many work flows and other processes.

When looking at the organisational hierarchy there is two things to consider. The first is matching the employees and sometimes some contractors against rules; a process outcome that will then need to be interfaced to all kind of systems through the IT directory systems and others.

The second and more complex item is the change in the organisation, which is at least happening somewhere in a normal sized enterprise at least fortnightly.

Here you should remember that some mangers will not just create a new team in the existing organisational levels but suddenly start to introduce a new level (for example put a project manager between himself a some part of his/her team) as this will make them more important (a manager defines his influence on the numbers of hierarchies below him). If that happens, your systems (I do not only mean the HR system) will need to cope with this. This is where a change in business will create some problems in directories and work flow systems straight away. So when setting up the employee master data management process do not forget this as I did in the first time.

5.3.1.6.2 Leave management

Leave management is a simple enough process on holidays, sickness, paternity, etc. and is often even performed on an Excel sheet. The added complexity is that all this information needs to be interfaced to many other systems, that the manager will be to be informed and that there is a great need on reports in area.

Also note that leave management systems require to have a credit account on annual leave, needs a document storage system for sick notes from the MD and a warning system if the threshold on days of sickness is reached in terms of actions to reduce the salary.

5.3.1.6.3 Visa processing

When I first encountered this process I thought of a mistake that this process should be done in travel management.

However visa processing is a process requiring very confidential data and is required at least in 40 countries to be done outside of the normal travel management. Visas often also require a special guarantee from the enterprise and are easier to obtain for employees that belong to a well known enterprise. In most countries this is also still a manual process as most embassies have no remote service for this.

5.3.1.6.3 Time and attendance

Recording time together with payroll is also one of the oldest processes in IS and it therefore astonishing how many mistakes are still done with it.

When recording time there is no system that fits all cases as time recording in an IS department is very different to an oil rig where every minute not on the job costs huge amounts. So it is always good to step back and a proper job in looking at all the factors involved before implementing a system. Also the trust in entering the right number of hours is very different why in some cases a time recording system with RFID's makes sense, while for a mobile sales force this may just prove a very counterproductive way.

Additional for all interfaces you should always remember that you may need to submit time in two formats one decimal and the other in hours and minutes as time is recalculated in money and accountancy is very precise. So 20 minutes may be .33 or 0:20. The problem always occurs when some smart architect will just try to do an automatic conversion that will then record 19 Minutes instead and subsequently the related invoice is rejected.

5.3.1.6.4 **ESS/MSS**

Any changes to non organisational master data, visa and leave can be done in employee & management self service, time and attendance only when it makes sense. All the other activities should only be attempted after a very careful critical analysis.

5.3.1.7 Separation management

Separation Management is the last level 2 process in the Hire-to-Retire process and is a relative simple process.

The important thing on this process is always to remember that once an employee separates from the enterprise he/she has no longer access to self service functions. This may sound stupid as a note, but I have seen it done wrong so many times that I just want to point it out anyhow.

5.3.1.7.1 Data management

When an employee leaves the enterprise it is important that a lot of data is updated. In the first instance this involves the same items as for a new hire just in reverse.

Second at leaving the enterprise the system will need to produce a feed to the pension system to inform it that the pension company needs to take over or in the case of a benefit defined pension the enterprise own pension fund. I the same way the health and welfare policies will need to be cancelled.

Finally the system will to produce all the legal forms required and inform the revenue services.

So this process requires a lot of internal & external interfaces.

5.3.1.7.2 Clearance

Joining an enterprise often requires as much security clearance as to leave the company; sometimes the leaving actually requires more clearance as many staffs that leave a company have a lot of knowledge, such as customer data, engineering data, intellectual property, etc.

Sometimes people are actually head hunted away because of their specific knowledge or customer contacts even if they are in breach of their contract. This is also why if sales people are terminated they are given 5 minutes under supervision to clear their desk.

So the exit clearance has to ensure that staffs are aware that their actions will be monitored and that they cannot use any intellectual property or confidential information gained while they were employed. At the same time it is important to ensure that all passwords and clearance are revoked, for this a good interface architecture is essential.

5.3.1.7.3 Exit interview

Sometimes exit interviews are done in half baked way with most people not knowing what happened in the interview just after 5 minutes. It is therefore important to keep the exit interview data with the master data of leaving employees with all the references to their knowledge and other useful information so that the data can be found again specifically if the replacement has not yet arrived. It is also important to add any new residential address of the leaving staff in the system.

5.3.2 Customer contact to resolution

This high level process is is also called customer service and as such it is applicable to all enterprises and public organisations.

However some organisations have often problems in defining their customers, this definition work needs to be completed before starting to implement this process or parts thereof.

At this point it should be noted that no process adoption can ever solve the problem of not defining areas such as customers or business partners on an enterprise wide level.

Up to 10 years ago there was a level 2 process on "In House Repair" in this level 1 process. Given the situation that repairs are done less often than replacements and even the change that today they are usually performed on customer site I have dropped this process.

5.3.2.1 Service order management

Within customer contact to resolution there are three major processes to handle customer service.

The first one is the service order based one where a service order is created when the customer contacts the enterprise. The order in term can be handled in lieu or a payment is agreed with the customer. The order as such is important as to follow the customer requirement through and to attach all the require resource allocation (such as time & material) it represents the financial reference.

The second one is the service contract where a customer has an agreement with the enterprise for support him/her on defined requirements.

Both these ways of capturing service requests from the customers need to be predefined before starting an effective customer service, as the service execution will otherwise always get in trouble as the service requests are not logged properly and there will always be the question on financials associated with resolving the service request.

The third one is finally the warranty process where all of the defined costs will be booked against the warranty cost centre.

So in Service Order management we are looking at individual service requests or a defined group.

5.3.2.1.1 Service order

The first process is to define the service order as such. In this process it is important to design templates for service orders that are likely to be processed and to determine possible work flows. A good practise is also to include a business rule engine here to adapt the order in a dynamic way.

At this stage it also important to define all the important dependencies so that the later processing can be done automatically as much as possible.

5.3.2.1.2 Quotation service

Once a customer contacts the enterprise with a request first a decision if the request is handled in goodwill should me made. The decision on this should ideally be handled in a workflow or an empowerment for the representative on goodwill. The customer service representative needs to inform the customer of an anticipated result with time or date. A workflow should only be attempted if the customer insists on goodwill and an agreement cannot be reached.

If the customer request is not covered by goodwill the quotation service as such needs to be started with asking the customer on the details of the request and the desired time to resolution. Standard quotations should be processed automatically (since 98 % of requests should be reoccurring). Only for the minority of quotation there should be a work flow in place.

5.3.2.1.3 Order processes

Once the quotation is accepted by the customer (in a normal setting this happens about 45 seconds after the customer contacts the enterprise) the details will be confirmed and if there is no goodwill case the payment details will be recorded.

If the customer is known to be credit worthy (interface with Finance) or if the order is paid directly the order will be processed, otherwise an invoice is issued and the order is put on hold until AR will report on the incoming payment.

5.3.2.1.4 Service employee resource planning

Once the service order is confirmed this process will ensure that the employees that are required to process the service request are earmarked for this task and not double booked on other business. So here it may be good to have interfaces to all the other systems that will plan the time of the same pool of employees.

If staff is not available for the service request an escalation will need to be started and the customer informed.

Ideally this process should also check on potential supplies on material, however in real life the materials are often first known when the request is well under way.

5.3.2.1.5 Service confirmation processing

Once the resources are planned the customer will need to receive a detailed confirmation with the details of the person handling his/her request.

At the same time a confirmation is also required to inform the agent responsible for the order to update her/his work plan as well as a note to her/his manager.

5.3.2.1.6 Product service letter processing

I have long pondered on how to call this process, as it could also be called Service or Product Service Letter Processing instead, but then I decided against it, because it has too much of Service in it.

This process is important so that there is a record of the service order performed against a certain product or service. This information in term may show to a single bad behaviour or to a bad lot or even a whole line of products or services. This information in term is then often used for product recalls and process improvement.

Additionally it might also be used if another request is processed on that product to spot similarities or just as a part of the product history. In term of Services the process is used in the health sector on surgeries to spot patterns or simply to warn the surgeon that a similar condition was already treated before.

5.3.2.1.7 Logistics integration processes

With every service order it is also important to ensure the integration into logistics to ensure that the service order is not delayed.

5.3.2.1.8 Service order analytics

Service Order Analytics are a vital part not only for the tasks performed, logistics prediction, resource planning and the management procedures, but as mentioned beforehand they can often also show improvements and major shortfalls in the enterprise.

The analytics are also used to create FAQ and standard manuals on reoccurring service orders.

5.3.2.2 Service contract management

As mentioned before service contract management looks at the process when a customer has made special provisions with the enterprise to receive support in a certain area.

This process is also the main income for many businesses and as such is pretty important. Examples for this are most software companies and specially the open source enterprises.

5.3.2.2.1 Service agreement

The first process is the service agreement that will cover all the legal provisions and ideally implement them into templates that are interfaced into all the resulting processes. This kind of automatic setup will serve your enterprise very well as most companies will only have 1 or 2 potential service agreements on a product or service line.

5.3.2.2.2 Service contract quotation processing

Service contracts are usually priced on a quantity (e.g. number of users) or a mix of quantities (ERP vendors are very good at that game). Additional some discounts may be offered through negotiations.

The contracts are usually also set up in a way that they will renew on an annual basis with a 30 day window for cancellations or for price increases (seldom decreases).

This is why the Service Contract Quotation Processing is done in iteration with different discounts and a different mix of quantities until both sides can agree on a deal.

5.3.2.2.3 Service contract processing

Once a service contract is accepted and signed it will be processed for financials, who will set the customer and agree the payments. For Service Contract Processing it is important to get the agreement from Finance to continue with the Service Contract Processing.

At this point a project management template will be initiated with the quantities from the order and start with some resource allocation.

5.3.2.2.4 Usage based contract management

If the service contract is based on an agreed usage of resources the automatic generated project template will need to be executed. Sometimes a usage contract is also combined with an in-sourcing agreement which makes this straight forward process very complicated. In that case it is important to create a close working interface with the Hire-to-Retire process that will ensure that the in-sourced resource remains allocated to the contract in question. So far as I am aware there are no standard solutions for this, however please contact me if you are aware of any.

5.3.2.2.5 Service Level Management

The Service Level Management that I have discussed in great detail before for IS needs to implemented at this point. As I given all the EPC in detail I will revisit this here.

5.3.2.2.6 Value and quantity contracts

There is a special kind of service contract that can often be encountered in facility Management and Information Services called Value and Quantity Contract. These contracts are more or less prepaid work or consultancy agreements for a given period. So from a process view they fall between the Service Order and the Service Contract or are often misused for other work and just budgeted on the service accounts.

It is highly advisable to keep them in a separate process and only allocate them to a specific process when needed as they might otherwise mess up many other processes and resource allocations.

5.3.2.2.7 Contract determination

Contract Determination is a wonderful word for a process that is really focussing on the legal side of contracts. Since service contracts will often need to be agreed in detail by lawyers it is important to touch on the process behind this as lawyers will otherwise charge your enterprise huge amounts.

Contract Determination consist briefly on the following tasks: Purpose, Policy, Background, Contract Time Determination, Rates, other influencing factors, adapting circumstances to heighten rates, scheduling, recording and invoicing, techniques on time and material calculations, conclusion, transition & considerations.

Once the legal teams have captured and agreed all these facts they need to be re transferred into the service contract management, which is hard task as lawyers are not known for firm commitment language.

5.3.2.2.8 Service plan processing

Once everything is set up a service plan or service project plan is established from the previous steps. In this process the plan is now executed. During the execution it might happen that this process will need an own processing system.

I will discuss these processing systems in the chapter on "Case management". This process could therefore also be described as the master for case management.

5.3.2.2.9 Service contract analytics

As Service Contracts are often the major part of the income of an enterprise, analytics on the contracts become that more important. So the analytics here are mainly on resource allocation, income, earnings per contract, customer satisfaction and profitability analysis.

5.3.2.3 Complaints & returns

When working for a service company you might ignore this process, however a service is due for complaints as well as a product it is often just called another name.

On return you are however quite right as they only attach to an unwanted product unless the service order or contract has yet not started or you are in a cooling off period.

5.3.2.3.1 Knowledge management

When processing any complaint a key ingredient is the knowledge of a similar case happening before and the solution for it as this will usually answer most of the complaints and reduce the number of return as well as filter the easy cases.

One of the areas on Knowledge Management from an architecture perspective is speed and precision. The whole process needs to enable the service representative to find the right answer in a very fast time (under 20 seconds).

All systems that will not accomplish this even if they are superior in almost everything else should not be used as it will almost always lead to the complaint uphold or the goods returned even if a solution can be found after some time. This is a bit different in some countries where the customers are used to bad services and are used to hold on waiting lines.

5.3.2.3.2 Complaints processing

Any complaint first need to logged and then classified in terms of the service levels and in terms of the next steps. For this the service representative will need a system with template processes for almost all possible cases. These need to include the service levels that the complaint is about as well as a work flow for further processing.

The customer needs to be given a reference as well the contact details of the allocated person and an estimate on when his/her complaint will be followed up, unless the service representative can answer the complaint from the knowledge management system straight away and the customer accepts the resolution.

5.3.2.3.3 Returns processing

The Returns Processing process will first require the service representative to check for the eligibility of the return, for this the system will need to be configured with clear business rules. Additional a certain allowance on goodwill need to be provided.

The next step is to identify the return. If the product in question is of low value and high transport costs or if the product is not resalable the process may even consist of weaving the return process and still crediting for a return. In most cases however the product needs to be shipped back to the company and transportation agreed. The service representative will also need to inform the customer on how the product needs to arrive (packaging and quality).

Once the product arrives back at the warehouse in the agreed condition with the return reference the account of the customer will be credited with the return value.

5.3.2.3.4 Follow-up processes

Every customer complaint, even those solved before need to be followed up to ensure a high customer satisfaction (often a key KPI).

By following up a complaint the process will run as long as possible until the customer will close it or a very senior manager will do so.

This is important as most dissatisfaction comes from closing complaints early and often just sending a canned response (of course there are few exceptions on enterprises that are not keen on customer service).

If the complaint is likely to get to a court it is important to predefine a workflow involving the in-house legal consolers. At that point the case will be noted as transferred to legal and as the case may come back afterwards it should not be archived before finally closing it.

5.3.2.3.5 Recall management

Recall Management is a special case of the return process. This process starts with either informing the customer on a recall if his/her address is known or by issuing press releases and advertisements informing customers on the recall.

All costs for recalls need to be handled separately to a dedicated cost code. The reason behind this is that every company will put money aside for recalls and classify them as a special expenditure.

This has often led to creative accounting in the past by parking money on a good year and releasing it on a bad year, saving taxes and falsifying the income reports.

This is the reason why the funds for recalls are monitored very closely by the revenue and other regulators and all costs need to be kept strictly apart.

All recalled products will need to be classified as such so that they are classified as recalled, unless the recalled product (e.g. a car) can be fixed. In that case the recall management will arrange for this to happen, by issuing service orders to other service companies or retailers of their product with the names of the customers.

5.3.2.3.6 Warehouse management integration

Any returned or recalled product will arrive at the warehouse where one of three things will happen. After a quality check (even important on faulty products to determine if the fault has already happened) the product will either be recycled (or destroyed), put into a special warehouse location classified as used good or reassigned to the new stock. In some cases the goods will require a "polishing up" process or repacking process as determined in the quality check.

5.3.2.3.7 Logistics integration

It is required that the return and recall process is integrated in the overall logistic process to avoid higher costs. For example if possible to collect a return while delivering an order can save on logistic costs. All those determinations will however be done in the logistics process.

5.3.2.3.8 Financial integration

As mentioned before in the recall process it is very important to allocate the costs of all the processes to separate cost centres allowing ensuring the legal requirements as well as the reporting on cost centres for profitability.

5.3.2.3.9 Complaints and returns analytics

The analytics in this area need to be auditor proof in the extreme, so this why all the development for a data warehouse set up need to be approved by all stakeholders. The main part is recall management that needs often even to be certified by the financial regulators or the revenue.

5.3.2.4 Case management

Case management is a process that records all interactions on business case basis. It is most used in the health and legal sector, however it also central for the customer contact to resolution process in terms of the means to follow up all customer interaction. It is often the process delivering service contracts. In IS it is also called the service operation management process.

It is nowadays often incorporated in ERP or CRM systems, but it is also available as a stand alone system. This needs however be attached with a word of warning as due to a misunderstanding some analysts in the last years have mixed it up with BPM tools which have NO place in this straight forward process.

5.3.2.4.1 Case processing

In the heart of case management is the case processing that starts with a request based on a service contract, a service order, warranty, return, complaint or recall.

It then follows to classify the request against the service levels and is used to record all activities performed until the request or case is satisfactory closed.

Later it is used as the tool for auditing the case or to retrieve information on an earlier case. Case processing is organised primary on the individual customer, but secondary also organised in groups of cases. The groups are always specific to the industry and the specifics in that industry. A group in health could be all motion related cases with a specific on knee surgery.

The process will also store all the associated information.

5.3.2.4.2 Change request management

Once a request is not covered by the predefined service levels it is either withdrawn or it becomes a change request. The change request process in case management will follow the same way as change request in IS. They will be impacted and submitted to a Change Authority Board (CAB) where a decision will be reached on its implementation, rejection or transfer to negotiation for a new service order or change to the existing service contract with the customer.

5.3.2.4.3 Service confirmation processing

All the previous mentioned service processing was on an order or contract basis, the service requests however will processed via the case management, so that confirmations on individual requests will be issued from the case management process to the parties defined in the service and operational agreements.

5.3.2.4.4 Activity processing

Within case management it may get to the point that activities are required which span more than the usual cases. Such activities may include questionnaires or other activities that are required by a group of cases. This process is pretty important when processing many cases in recall management.

Activity Processing therefore requires a clear access management and needs to be interlinked with the case being processed.

5.3.2.4.5 Supporting processes

Since case management is a process to administer all interactions on business case basis with the customer contact to resolution process it needs to be connected to other processes that will be used to resolve the customer request.

Here it is important to interface if possible, but if not to create simple supporting processes. For example if a heavy machinery is recalled and cannot be repaired on site but needs to dissembled there may not be an existent process for dissembling a used system, so in that case a supporting process will need to be created to assist in this endeavour.

5.3.2.4.6 Case management analytics

The analytics in case management will need to create reports on the numbers of cases, the number of change requests and the speed in which they are processed against the service levels.

Additionally reports on open cases, any escalation, risk, issues discovered and the change request status and progression are required.

Ideally there should also be a prediction system in place to plan for future resource allocation.

5.3.2.5 Warranty management

Within this process a warranty is an assurance by one party to the other party that if certain facts or conditions are true or will happen, the other party is permitted to rely on that assurance and seek some type of remedy if it is not true or followed. This process is not about the warranty deed in real estate.

The warranty process is also separate from the goodwill as the warranty needs to follow very strict routes, while the goodwill is not an assurance.

5.3.2.5.1 Customer and vendor warranty

Before starting any warranty processing the customer and vendor warranty process will define the warranty towards the customer of the enterprise as well as the vendors warranty assurance to the enterprise. This in itself is required so that any warranty processing can take place and in the case of a retailer this is the most important process as warranties are just handed from customer to vendor and vice versa. If the enterprise extends the vendors warranty this process will define the rules to operate.

The second part of the process is to handle the warranty operational procedures. This could for example mean that if it is not possible to repair or replace the unit the customer will receive a refund that he can only spent on other products similar to the one handed over for warranty processing.

5.3.2.5.2 Product and warranty registration

To process warranties products and some very small way services will need to be registered for warranty to determine the start of the warranty period. If the product is resold in retail this need to happen at the point of the ultimate seller. As this sometimes proves complicated some enterprises will ask the end customer to send or register the product on the web direct with them.

Many enterprise use the warranty registration as a cross selling exercise. Even if this annoys many customers it will provide the enterprise with a nice additional income and keep the warranty registrations at a minimum. It is therefore important to allow the process to be designed to offer this additional cross selling.

It should also be pointed out that it is a bad idea to implement an auto-registration feature as products often take a long time from the manufacturer to the end reseller via many intermediaries. In some circumstances a bulk registration feature should be offered if the products are likely to be bought by the end customers in bulk.

5.3.2.5.3 Warranty determination

Warranty determination is all about the fine legal process, where all the details of a warranty agreement will be produced and implemented into a warranty determination system, as most warranties need to be processed automatically to keep the overhead costs at a minimum.

The warranty determination process will also describe the warranty net exposure per case to the enterprise by subtracting the vendor warranty determination from the customer warranty determination.

5.3.2.5.4 Warranty claim processing

Finally if a warranty case is submitted the warranty claim process should be able to determine in a very short period if the claim is valid.

If the claim not valid the process will need to be designed to help the customer service representative explaining why this is the case and communicate this to the customer. It should be noted that refusing claims often will cost the enterprise more money than to progress, so an analysis needs to determine the level in which a goodwill gesture will save a higher exposure.

If the claim is valid the process needs to determine the next steps such as an on-site visit, a return of the unit (transfer to the return process for logistic) for repair, recycling or a simple non return. This is than followed up by the operational process for compensation set out in the former processes.

If the unit is required to be repaired on site or in-house there is the need for supporting processes that are described in the case management process.

5.3.2.5.5 Warranty analysis

The main analytics required for the warranty process are the operational reports, the costs on the actual warranties, the net present and expected exposure cost per product line and per cost centre.

5.3.3 Plan to Produce

Plan to Produce is a process that is designed and operated by engineers making it very difficult to describe it to level that anyone would consider complete.

The "Plan to Produce" process that you will find here is the traditional process. Within the last 10 years more and more enterprises have tried to implement a similar process called Product Lifecycle Management.

Product Lifecycle Management tries to capture a plan to produce process in much more detail and consists similar to this process of four level 2 processes with the associated level 3 processes. These are:

Conceive

Consisting of imagine, specify, plan and innovate

Design

Consisting of describe, define, develop, test, analyze and validate

Realize

Consisting of use, operate, maintain, support, sustain, phase-out, retire, recycle and disposal

Service

Consisting of communicate, manage and collaborate

The main reason why in the standard processes I still refer to the older P2P process is that despite of spending billions on implementing the new integrated PLM process the results are not very encouraging as most companies will find that this process proves to be over complicated and does not offer any positive ROI case even if the business benefits are realistically quite high. Most enterprises are still managing the conceive phase separately as a project and the service phase in the customer contact to resulting processes. Even processes such as the retirement and the material recycling or disposals are often separately managed.

At a later stage when the process is established with a positive ROI in more than 75 % of its implementations I might describe this process in detail as well, but that will most certainly take more than a few pages.

5.3.3.1 Production planning

The plan to produce process will start with the production planning even if it would be more logical to start with the product development process. This is due to history which I am trying to change here.

5.3.3.1.1 Production planning

Production planning starts with the capture of the customer demand and the planning decision on the production model required. The demand is almost always derived from studies on potential and lost sales conducted by marketing and sales. On the side of the production model most enterprises use either the Lot size model developed by H.M. Wagner and T.H. Whitin in 1958 or the Quadratic Cost Model and Linear Decision Rule by Holt, Modigliani, Muth and Simon in 1960 for the Pittsburgh Paint Company. Both models come with a large amount of related refinement models; however they all have the benefit that they are based on a solid formula rather than on an idea only, like many more modern researches into production planning. As such they are still used as the basis for most production planning systems nowadays.

The next step in the production planning process is based on the concept planning hierarchies to decide on the decision in order of their importance.

This is followed by the cost calculation and the resource planning that is usually combined with an iterative time horizon calculation.

Most product planning is done on a unit aggregate level, however if the planning involves more complex products a planning is done on a hierarchical product structure.

Please note that most of the process in product planning is closely governed by mathematical models.

5.3.3.1.2 Capacity planning

Once the production planning process is finished with its calculations the capacity in terms of the production resource and materials need to started and planned.

The capacity planning process in production does really differ from that of project planning only that the production planning algorithms provide a much more detailed input.

The capacity management process then is also required to be manipulated by certain external factors such as plant maintenance periods or unforeseen events such as strikes.

5.3.3.1.3 Financial integration

The production planning process will need to be both integrated as a process into the financial management as well as to the parameters defined in the process to determine the planned costs for each product and the associated bill of materials.

5.3.3.2 Manufacturing execution

Manufacturing is part of the plan to produce process but may actually not happen at the same enterprise where the other processes are performed and should therefore always be designed in a way easily detachable from the rest. This in itself is also often the reason why the fully integrated PLM does not deliver.

Assuming that most manufacturing is taking place at the most efficient side it is important that not too many assumptions toward the executing process and system are made. The main part of the process is therefore geared toward information exchange, control and supervision.

5.3.3.2.1 Manufacturing execution

This process is really the execution of the decision reached in product planning. The process is a one of effort that is usually done as a project

5.3.3.2.2 Shop floor integration

Shop Floor Integration is the main process within the manufacturing execution. Paper is still the most common way for manufacturers to collect production data. The shop floor integration process is intended as the antidote to this malfunction.

The idea is to collect all the data of manufacturing; however the workable solution is looking more to record data at the end of a defined stage and then record the process as well as the time spent.

Stages in this setting are defined as a set of activities on one production unit, so that the time spent also reflects the amortisation of that unit.

Most Shop Floor Integration systems consist out of a very basic setup, which is done as follows for small series or discrete products as an example:

1. Print of a product order with production lines that are specifying the execution in term of steps and materials required. The print will have a bar-code with the production order and is assigned to a worker who will have a bar-code with his personnel number. Once he/she receives the order he/she will scan the personal bar-code and then the bar-code of the production order

2. The worker will next move to collect the materials with scanning the bill of material as bar-code and consequently the work order

3. On each stage of the manufacturing the worker will then always scan the work order on each production unit at the start and at the end

4. If additional supplies are needed (a unit damaged a part during the process) the material will be handed out the same way as in step 2

5. Finally he/she will scan the completed unit and return any left materials

6. The finalised products are the registered against the work order and marked

7. The quality control officer will then also start scanning his personal bar-code and the work order. If there are any quality rejects the products are marked and entered in the system associated to the work order.

The information will then be either submitted back to the main production planning systems within the enterprise or to the enterprise that has outsourced the manufacturing.

5.3.3.2.3 Supervision and control

In manufacturing there is the need to supervise the quality control of the manufacturing unit independently, especially if it is outsourced.

This process is usually done by random secondary quality controls when the finished products reaches the warehouse and monitoring the quality controls of the company according to the total quality control guidelines. The guidelines will measure the maturity of the process according to ISO 9001 or other accepted frameworks. The inspections and random check will be recorded and compared to the SLA. If there are any discrepancies the process will need to escalate them

5.3.3.3 Product development

Product Development is one test best documented processes, a very good description together with a complete process description can be found at http://en.wikipedia.org/wiki/New_product_development .

This is also the reason why I will not linger in process description as I do not want to fill the book with a copy and paste approach but instead want to fill the gaps.

5.3.3.3.1 Product development

My observation in working in this area have thought me that the product development is best run as a project activity with many supporting processes that can be re-utilized from other process such as cost estimation, resource management or scheduling. It is seldom intelligent to produce one large system in product development, as the product development takes place with so many different roles that (industry espionage as reason) the right kind of access management for an integrated system will either fail or severely disrupt the creative approach need in a successful product development.

5.3.3.3.2 Development collaboration

Within the product development departments there is always the tendency to start with a lot of collaboration tools, as well as a lot of paper with only a few using one system. When the next large development starts the process repeats as in the beginning there is lots of budget and management is keen not to dampen the enthusiasm.

This almost always leads to many obsolete systems and the problem of finding anything afterwards. So the main best practise in this area is not to find the best user acceptable tool, but instead create a system that can easily scan all the papers and has a good meta data management in reading handwritten notes to make them searchable as well as a system that is good in emptying the data store of other system to archive the material and make it searchable. Any notion to try to come up with the ultimate master system will be very likely flawed.

5.3.3.4 Lifecycle data management

Plan to Production is all about data that however is often lost even if the investment has been huge to arrive at it. An example of this can be found in many laboratory trials to find that special substance that is needed by the market right now. After finding the successful product however often all the other data that might contain an answer for a market demand that is cropping up next year is often lost or severely compromised.

All the life cycle data always need to be guarded as it is the intellectual property of a company that can often not be protected in its entirety through patent and other IP tools, but must rely on secrecy.

5.3.3.4.1 Document management

All documents need to be managed, however as I have stated in development collaboration it is not always possible to dictate a central or even a suite of document management systems. So the process of document management in the first place is to create a document retrieval system that will even work if no meta-data is entered in the system.

This in itself may sound trivial and just seen as an excuse; however in product research often people will search for previous material with a complete different question in mind. So if someone has added a document containing chemical trials with the meta data "plant fertilizer" in the system and someone is looking on research for one of the formulas contained in that document to create an anti wrinkle cream he/she is not likely to find it unless the system is indexed on a free search algorithm instead of a meta data based one. In the data architecture that most likely means the difference of a system based on a column orientated database rather than a relational database model.

5.3.3.4.2 Product structure management

Product structure data consists of materials (called bill of material (BOM)), their assemblies (including sub- assemblies), configuration, variants and relationships.

For all these groups of data there are 5 main views that will show a different picture in each view of the product. The views are: Service View, Design View, Purchasing View, Manufacturing View and the Sales & Marketing View.

So within the product structure management all these information's with their distinct views need to be managed and interfaced. So if the marketing department updates its view on variants of a product it is important that that information never is actively used in manufacturing execution process even if the data is labelled exactly the same.

5.3.3.4.3 Recipe management

Recipes Management will follow the same process as the Product Structure Management just with different wordings and with added chemical process data category.

5.3.3.4.4 Specification management

Specifications are a similar interesting subject on data as they are also given in different views. These views are that the specification is given in absolute numbers, in variable numbers, as a reference to a norm or in is described in association to another specification (e.g. like M67537, just 1mm longer).

So here again it is important that the right process gets the right information.

5.3.3.4.5 Change and configuration management

Changes, as well as configurations on a product need to be managed in the plan to produce data management not with the classical change process, but they need to be exactly recorded (audit proof) and often countersigned (four eyes principle).

5.3.4 Campaign to Sale

This process is often also described as marketing. It is important to recognise that this process is not only important for organisations that sell services or products against competition, but to support any kind of business activity (e.g. NGO's).

So the process or parts of it are important to everyone who will for example try to sell an idea or perform any kind of stakeholder management. I have seen part of the process even implemented in IT departments.

5.3.4.1 Marketing resource management

The first level 2 process is about planning the resources that in marketing can be quite costly, just think of the cost of a TV ad I prime time. This is also the reason that a great deal of process work is spent in this area.

The goal on this process is to gain market share and improve customer retention. Some ERP products also claim that it will speed the time to market; however I have not seen to many indications how this helps in the process. When talking about marketing most professionals in that area will always tell you that they acknowledge that 70 - 90 % of the money is spent on areas without any ROI, however the whole point of this process is to spend the money more effective.

To accomplish the higher effectiveness the process will concentrate on analysis, planning, development, implementation and measurements from an operational as well as from the financial view.

5.3.4.1.1 Market research

Market research is an analytical process that will perform investigations on external and internal data to the enterprise.

As such it is a process that is best performed with a statistical data warehouse system to follow market trend and to document them. It is important that market research will never come up with new untested ideas, but always be used to analyse current and historical demand. So if your enterprise is planning to introduce a ground breaking new technology that has not been presented before it is important not rely on this process. However that scenario is very seldom.

5.3.4.1.2 Budget planning

Wherever money is spent there is a budget to control the costs. So the first task in the process is to create a high level marketing plan to establish the scope of the activity and to identify the budget required to execute the plan.

5.3.4.1.3 Scenario planning

Scenario planning is another analysis process that is based on simulations to run potential marketing scenarios through an artificial intelligence. This planning on scenarios should be feed with the real market data collected through the market research. Often the simulations will achieve a great deal of better spent as they simulate the spent against different ideas.

5.3.4.1.4 Marketing planning and budgeting

So once the budget is released the process will focus to now create the actual marketing plan that is based on the agreed and released budget. Often the plan is based on a chosen scenario that has been simulated before.

At this process it is important to enter the marketing plan into the system to associate tasks and milestone of the plan against cost controls so that the budget can be released in a controlled way.

5.3.4.1.5 Budget control

The budget control takes place after the budget is released. At that point the first task is to adjust the real detailed level marketing plan to the actual released budget, as it is very seldom that the full requested budget is released.

Once the real budget has been adjusted to the plan the process needs to maintain the plan and actual against the revenue and the costs.

5.3.4.1.6 Product and brand planning

Since there are often different products and sometimes different brands for an enterprise this process is in place to coordinate all the efforts so that there is no collision on the marketing. This process is therefore always owned by the head of marketing and therefore usually only performed once a year together with the marketing strategy review,

The marketing strategy and its output are often also captured in this process, however marketing strategy as such I have never seen performed as a standard process.

5.3.4.1.7 Cost and volume planning

Given the fact that in all businesses there is a potential cost saving on purchasing volumes instead of individual items or services, it is very important to combine all the activities in the various product or service brands into a central purchasing pool to get the best deals and as such hopefully the best ROI (since the ROI is based on the cost and benefit the only concern of this process is the cost, so a ROI reduction is helped but not fully accomplished by this process).

5.3.4.1.8 Marketing plan analysis

The plan analysis is a process that is non-operational and will pick up on all the ongoing activities on a detailed level to improve the future panning and execution. This process could therefore also be described as service and operations improvement process. From an architecture perspective an analytical data warehouse is of great help in supporting the process with 24 h feeds from all the sales related systems.

5.3.4.1.9 Marketing calendar

The marketing calendar process is the most important level 3 process in marketing planning and is also used often by non marketing processes such as in stakeholder management in IS.

The marketing calendar process that is sometimes sub divided into journals coordinating and controlling all marketing activity and reminding all involved, on upcoming topics. The marketing calendar process in smaller enterprises as well as if the process is used in non marketing areas is often implemented on calendar systems on the enterprise email and calendar system, in larger enterprises it is often part of the CRM system that is then again integrated into the personal email and calendar system.

The marketing calendar process will look at the status of every marketing activity and act as the project management tool for the overall process.

5.3.4.1.10 Marketing organisation

Marketing organisation is the process that will ensure that the list of cost centre and other approval holders is up to date

5.3.4.1.11 Workflow and approval

As there is a huge amount of money spent in marketing all approvals are handled through workflow ensuring that the marketing budget is released both as fast and as secure as possible.

5.3.4.2 Segmentation & list management

Market segmentation is used in marketing to divide the market into separate groups that can easier be targeted. The lists are then used for every segment to capture all the information held on each individual customer. In terms of online marketing the segmentation lists are often also based only on identifiers such as IP addresses or email addresses.

5.3.4.2.1 Multiple data source access

The multiple data source access process is another wording for a single marketing view in IS language.

The single view is not a trivial process to implement as it is implemented on a data warehouse system often with the need for master data management as well as almost in all enterprises even with the best of planning there are events that will create a heterogeneous data landscape (e.g. acquisitions & merger).

However it is important that IT needs to implement this as a one way access with a clear view on one system where marketing will then dump their version of the truth, so that the resulting data can then be seen as the true data for marketing, as the true customer data for production or sales may look different.

5.3.4.2.2 High speed data search

Marketing often need high speed data searches on their data instead of first raising a change request with IT. So this is why if marketing requires this process to set up a searchable database ideal in a column orientated format to enable the best results in speed. Instead of build a column orientated database there is always the possibility to by an appliance doing this.

5.3.4.2.3 Pre-filtered / personalized attribute lists

When trying to isolate lists of customers the "Pre-filtered / personalized attribute lists" process will first need to have a system that make it possible to store intermediary data, if that is not the case marketing will use Excel and often create a big mess for which IT is then automatically responsible.

This intermediary data is called pre-filtered data. Once the data is extracted marketing will try to apply attributes against the lists. Here IT needs to help with a scanning tool showing what kinds of attributes are present in how many data sets.

If that is not the case marketing will filter the data on attributes and then log a problem with the service desk as there seems no data matching if the attribute was set in table but never filled with data.

5.3.4.2.4 Sampling and splitting

Sampling and splitting is a quality assurance process in list management to randomly extract data on a source or to split the source in smaller parts (e.g. all customers' last names with V). The output is then used for trails to discover the quality of the data. The CRM system will need to have this feature.

5.3.4.2.5 Embedded predictive modelling

Once the sample data is tested it is sometimes of use to run a predictive modelling on it to ensure the data quality even further, Although I consider this as a standard process it is actually only implemented in a very few enterprises, as this kind of modelling will use very expensive resources with little extra benefit to show.

5.3.4.2.6 Personalised filters

Apart from attributes the data often also need to be filtered against some unpredictable attributes or combination thereof. The process is best accomplished with a DBA temporarily working with the marketing team writing customised code (SQL) to get the required data.

5.3.4.2.7 Quick counts

This process concentrates on running counts of data sets on all the associated systems, so if through the access of the marketing someone has identified 1000 customers the quick count process will tell how many of the feeding system contain what data count on that customer as sometimes there is one source clearly telling on high income of the customers, but for the customers in question the order system does not know the details as the customer has bought the product anonymous.

At this point it should also be pointed out that there is a constant struggle of marketing and sales. Sales will accept a customer with as little data as possible; as more data is just more work and often customers that are buying a product do not want to surrender all their personal data. On the other hand marketing can never get enough data on person making their life much easier.

5.3.4.2.8 Segment de-duplication

This process that is often not performed ensures that a customer chosen from segment in a marketing campaign is not included in another so that if the campaign is executed he/she is note targeted multiple times. The process is almost always done by a DBA.

5.3.4.2.9 Suppression filters

It happens that despite the best selection there is a negative selector for a segment as for example financial rating; this process will ensure to suppress the data sets from the segment even if all attributes are met. In this process however it very important not to violate the rules set out by compliance such as discrimination against gender or race. Even if marketing is asking for this IT is liable for such a breach of data manipulation in many legislations.

5.3.4.2.10 Target group optimisation

Once the lists have been created they are further optimised for the target group by combining the results with a feed from reference such as club memberships.

5.3.4.2.11 Clustering

After the list has been refined sometimes it is even refined once more by using the statistical method of clustering that will identify a homogenous group based on a set of given parameters, this process is mainly done if selling very specifically based products or services such as a wine cooler for 1000 bottles only to large specialised restaurants. This method is used very often in the tourism industry.

5.3.4.2.12 Data mining

Data Mining is properly the most misused word in IT as it used for a benefit description on all data related processes when there are no real benefits.

Data mining is the process to identify opportunities a in the data modelling process and is actually not done that often as it is very expensive to implement with a small return associated.

5.3.4.2.13 Decision trees

Decision trees is really a subset process of data mining with the benefit that it requires less investments, however with any good business rule system the benefits can be realised with far less investment, as decision tree techniques are easy to implement.

5.3.4.2.14 ABC analysis

ABC analysis is one of the more important processes as it focuses on the cost controlling and the calculation of the actual ROI. It is important to set up the activity based controlling at this stage to capture the costs in all activities before being able to calculate the benefit case.

5.3.4.2.15 List management - list format mapping

Once lists have been produced it is important to keep them as they represent a real commercial value for a given time. If the marketing campaign that builds on a list is going very well the lists are more important. Additional this process will also harmonise differences in the data fields such as truncated data from one source compared with non truncated or different versions of the same or similar address.

5.3.4.2.16 Duplicate checks

Even after de-duplication procedures it is important to check for duplicates as for example via name and address look for similar writing of names such as Karl or Carl

5.3.4.2.17 Postal validation

Sources such as the post office data on people moved (often with new address) are used to reduce the number of returns or misses.

5.3.4.2.18 Data cleansing

Any data provide by potential customers may be wrong. A classical area is address mining via the web where you need to leave address information before you can access some information.

So people who do not want to give their private data will enter Micky Mouse or Nosuchname in the City No-where. This is the kind of data that the process of data cleaning needs to find and eliminate as automatic system often cannot spot these patterns.

5.3.4.2.19 Data enrichment

The list data may now also be enriched with some data. This way it is possible make any marketing effort much more interesting, such as a search of address is combined with a list of road-shows. By using a Geographical Information Systems (GIS) the data can be enriched by pointing out the event or a specialised retailer near the potential customer with some directions for him/her.

5.3.4.2.20 List quality

This process finally is giving the report on all activity performed and has an embedded work flow that will initiate the lists to be authorised. This process is present in many enterprises as it will also show all the work performed to get to the list and stops people stopping the campaign as they have doubts on the quality of the data.

5.3.4.2.21 Lead and activity imports

At the final point the data is often further enriched by leads and activities supplied by external sources such as business partners. Since the enterprise will neither own the data or can vouch for the data the data will be just added

5.3.4.2.22 List analysis

The analysis reports on the list and segmentation management will show how much data is of what quality and how much data is available in what segments. Some of the analysis is then used back into the first process of market research where the marketing life cycle starts again.

5.3.5 Source to Pay (Procure to Pay)

This process has changed quite a bit during 1995 to 2005 from a process first driven on purchasing large bulk of materials at the highest discount or lowest price to get the best ROI. Nowadays the process has changed more to include the specific needs as well as a good supplier customer relationship. This level 1 process however does not include supplier management, which has grown to be its own level 1 process. This process is more about the tactical and operational while supplier management is more on the strategic and governance parts. For enterprise architects it is important that it makes very little sense to implement the supplier management process before at least reaching a CMMI level 3 maturity on the S2P "Source to Pay" process.

Within S2P the highest savings are realised by automation on the manual administration of a purchase as often it will cost more than the purchase amount itself. The other important trend is to keep the number of suppliers down as the administration per supplier can otherwise outstrip any potential cost savings in choosing an additional supplier.

5.3.5.1 Sourcing

Sourcing with negotiation is certainly the one area everyone would think of when describing purchasing as a department. It is important always to remember that sourcing needs to be a process in which procurement works together with the business owner that requires the goods or services.

A violation of this simple relationship is also the main reasons for the failure of the process, as if the business owner starts purchasing with the procurement professional often to get matters moving faster; the outcome is almost every time that it takes longer as he/she will have forgotten some important details.

298

On the other hand sourcing done purely by procurement professionals with a minimum of involvement of the business users ("just hand me over a short description what you need") will almost always led to ordering the wrong items, unless the item is very generic. Often IT professional including some architects will often push for procurement to control everything and only involve the business owners in a workflow as this is easier than coming up with a true collaboration system with many changes all the time.

5.3.5.1.1 Market / demand analysis

The process starts with the demand that could represent two things in the process, the first is clearly defined demand known and the other part is the potential demand that is best discovered by linking the S2P process with the market analysis from marketing and production planning.

5.3.5.1.2 Develop category strategy

Once the demand is established this process will create categories. There will always be a category for others as the categories are just intended to capture the big items that can be sourced in bulk, such as IT contractors (like myself) via a few preferred suppliers. The business owners will always start to try to label nearly everything as special ("sourcing an experienced enterprise architect cannot be done via the same agencies that supply the support staff"), but the strategically chosen categories in this process will give the guidance on what is considered to be sourced in bulks. The process to develop the categories will always require specialists rather than managers to decide on categories, as some items may sound very standard, but in real business operations they require a highly sophisticated bespoke specification such as drills that can be both nothing special and very special dependent on use.

Categories are also very important for IS as each category means an interface partner.

5.3.5.1.3 **Evaluate, negotiate and award**

Once the need is categorised the evaluation of suppliers will start. Nowadays there are two principal categories of suppliers. The first and traditional ones are supplying against a specification or a service level agreement; while the second category will be involved as business partners in sharing the costs, but then be awarded a part of the sales. This risk sharing sourcing that is used in many industries of course requires a very different set-up and should always be included in the sourcing process as the procurement often want to include this process as a possibility.

The process of negotiations and award is usually less IS relevant as it happen more on a document basis. All the terms of these documents however need to be stored in the ERP system.

Also always remember that there are often a few suppliers per category to ensure that there is still competition after a contract has been awarded and to ensure against complacency of suppliers.

5.3.5.1.4 Supplier performance management

Once a supplier is set up he needs to be monitored. The monitoring should always include parameters that were agreed in the service level agreement in the negotiations.

The monitoring techniques will first need to be validated with the supplier as the report of actual against contracted levels will only have a limited impact.

Enterprises may want to monitor other parameters as well; in that case always remember to keep them apart.

5.3.5.1.5 Contract compliance and savings validation

Apart from the performance management this process concentrates on compliance of the supplier that is done in an audit style agreed in the contracts as well looking at savings validated. Often if a supplier is given a contract the contract will state that during a fixed period the supplier will realise a certain percentage of savings; however this will only be done against certain categories and not if the supplier acts as a business partner sharing in the risk. So often I have seen a certain danger that an ERP package is just being implemented as the only true reflection of the standard business process with the result of destroying the purchasing strategy; so in this case it is beneficial to act a bit critical.

5.3.5.1.6 Supplier adoption

After a supplier is chosen this process will bring him on board, therefore this process is often also called "On-boarding". For IT this means the creation of an Extra-net where suppliers can find all the resources required, sometimes it even means access to the enterprise intranet and email system if the supplier shares in the risk and is also involved in decision making

5.3.5.1.7 Catalogue management and content management

Purchasing is all about Catalogues with content as they represent what is available from the supplier in question. Catalogues in purchasing are still often "punched out" of the supplier's web site. This technology works as a screen scrapping and even if XML and WS has been around for a long time the ISO norm still describes this older method of capturing catalogues.

The catalogues captured in table formats will then be transferred to an internal web shop system that will act as the internal ordering system with workflows against cost centre mangers on baskets as a form of authorisation. Of course the workflow needs to be configured to avoid that every petty item requires an authorisation. Once an order cross a threshold or after a defined time the items are ordered in bulk with supplier having to distribute the items to the individual requesters.

When importing catalogue items into the purchasing system it is always important to define where they are hold as the master record in the enterprise (material management in ERP vs. internal web shop system).

5.3.5.1.8 Contract management

Once a contract is signed with a supplier it needs constant management to ensure that any misunderstandings can be resolve quickly. This process will also need to include an own change management that can and shall be reused from other processes

5.3.5.1.9 Tactical / low value buying and fulfilment

Purchasing of low value items should be done via a pre-agreed budget that only requires random authorisation; once delivered the requester will need to acknowledge the items in a self service module, so that the item can be paid via direct debit or other means.

5.3.5.2 Invoice payment

The payment of any goods or services will always need to follow the three way matching process. So if an invoice arrives the order is first checked, if they match the payment will be authorised if the signed goods receipt or service receipt (e.g. timesheet) will match the order and the invoice. This is best way to ensure that payments are only done on ordered goods or services that have also arrived.

5.3.5.2.1 Assigning payment forms

The assignment process is a legal process to assign the benefits of a contract. It is a process with very little o no IT involvement

5.3.5.2.2 Scheduling payment runs

Payments were traditional done in batches called runs as they often ended in printing cheques or electronic payments on systems that only supported batch operations. However nowadays payments are still often done in runs. So if your enterprise still operates AP runs they need to be scheduled.

5.3.5.2.3 Discount realisation

Within the payment process discounts will often need to be applied, specifically discounts on early payments also called rebates.

5.3.5.2.4 Dynamic discount management

Sometimes the contracts come with a highly complicated structure on discounts that are often granted on certain minimum amounts on combined products, where it is cheaper for the enterprise to order more items than required and to then put them on hold until they are required in the future.

This kind of complex contract discounts will of course require a sophisticated system that is often build on a business rule engine to compensate for changes and enable an automatic process execution.

5.3.5.3 Invoice receipt & entry

Invoices can sometimes create a bit of a problem if they are written and sent before an order is raised. To avoid this it is best practise to demand the order number on the invoice and maybe even the receipt number making the 3 way matching process that easier.

5.3.5.3.1 Invoice receipt and scanning

Invoices are often still sent via post and then processed via scanning and OCR. All invoice systems should also acknowledge that many invoices arrive as pdf images on email attachments and also need to be scanned and put through OCR.

5.3.5.3.2 EDI invoices

Invoice from large suppliers are interfaced into the company either in old fashioned EDI format or as WS

5.3.5.3.3 Invoice verification and entry

Only invoices that agree with the minimum requirements set out by Finance will be accepted. Otherwise they will be rejected (e.g. missing order number).

5.3.5.4 Vendor management

Vendor management is kind of lightweight supplier management and if supplier management is implemented some of the processes may get obsolete.

5.3.5.4.1 Vendor master updates

The first process in this section will update any changes to vendor master data. As there are usually a lot of changes taking place it is advisable to offer this process as a self service.

5.3.5.4.2 Vendor help desk

Often small vendors create most work with the highest costs, so instead of providing them a phone service often a FAQ section with some training videos may help much more with the possibility for logging a request on a web page. This way the costs can be kept at a minimum.

5.3.5.4.3 **Supplier portal**

If your company requires many highly specialised small suppliers a supplier portal may be way to help the overall S2P process. The portal will offer the supplier a way to enter invoice, manage timesheets (contractors), create proposals on templates, manage documents and even be part of some workflows. Such a portal may then also benefit with a much easier way of integration.

5.3.5.4.4 **Vendor statement reconciliation**

This process describes the account balance between vendor and the enterprise, any resulting interest charges on advances, etc. and should be implemented using a standard ERP Financial packages

5.3.5.4.5 **P-Card / corporate card administration**

Many enterprises will supply managers with either specific purchasing cards (P-Card) or corporate credit cards. The process will make sure that all money spent is accounted for via the expense processing or open purchasing orders. In the case of the P-Card a two way matching against an order but without a goods receipt note is usually accepted practise.

5.3.5.4.6 Expense reports processing

Expenses are best capture in a self service, with receipts referenced send to a shared service centre or if they are in an electronic format uploaded for filling.

5.3.5.4.7 Expense reports audit

Only a few of the expense reports will then need to be audited to keep staff honest and alert. A random pick on 1 in 5000 is very normal unless there are indications of fraud with audits picks of 1 in 10.

However all receipts will need to be stored for the legal time and ideally scanned as some receipts are printed on thermal paper and will not be readable after a short time.

5.3.5.5 Invoice processing

The invoice processing will be fully automated. This process is almost always implemented against the standard on all tools I know about.

5.3.5.5.1 GL coding

All invoices need to be coded against the GL. If enterprises run more than one GL the Finance department needs to be asked against which one.

5.3.5.5.2 Approval management & matching

This process will execute the three way matching and initiate an approval work flow if the invoice exceeds a certain limit

5.3.5.5.3 Resolving match exceptions

Some exceptions on the amount of an invoice and the order may be automatically accepted. Usually this is due to rounding or because of fluctuations in an exchange rate and should best be resolved via a business rule system.

5.3.5.5.4 Discrepancy resolution

Discrepancies that can not otherwise be resolved need the manual attention of an AP clerk.

5.3.5.5.5 Price difference reconciliation

A specific discrepancy is on Unit price differences due to a price hike of the supplier. In this instance it is best first to try to automatically bounce the invoice back with a reference or best a copy of the order and only if this does not work to manually reconcile it.

5.3.5.6 Analytics & miscellaneous

This level 2 process contains items that are not clearly associated with other processes

5.3.5.6.1 MIS reporting

Purchasing requires a full set of reports that can be done in a data warehouse, however in the S2P process there is also the need for real-time reporting, for example on reconciliation.

5.3.5.6.2 Spend analytics

A very important analysis is the spent analysis that is running in the background and will trigger an escalation once it exceeds certain parameters. This is to ensure that the report is not used for micromanagement that will destroy motivation, but on the other hand will alarm the cost centre manager on irregularities.

5.3.5.6.3 Inter-company reconciliation's

Sometimes purchasing is done between companies that belong to the same enterprise. In that case there is the need for an inter-company reconciliation process.

5.3.5.6.4 **VAT reclaim**

VAT or Sales Tax is often paid on top of Invoices and will need to be reclaimed via this standard finance process.

5.3.5.6.5 **Month-end AP-GL reconciliation**

It is important that the AP and GL are reconciled at the end of the month so that Finance can close the month.

5.3.6 Sales

Sales in itself is one of the best areas to use the standard business process mainly due to the fact that most of the senior managers in that area have a great absence of process knowledge and as such are usually happy to collect suggestions by the knowledgeable enterprise architect.

Sales in itself is an area where they usually have an internal sales administration with very little to say and a sales force that is mainly interested in reaching targets and as too concerned about the wider picture. Since most sales mangers are ex members of the sales force themselves they often see themselves as motivators rather than as business owners. If the enterprise architect will wait for a great deal of input he has got a large problem on hand, however if she/he uses this processes by explaining them he/she will have an easy life. So this is why the knowledge of this process is so much more important than the record to report or the order to cash as those live in areas where the business owners are quite knowledgeable themselves.

5.3.6.1 Sales planning & forecasting

The first level 2 process touches on the area that is limited to the upper sales executives in the enterprise. At this point is often important to state that in sales people often get very high titles even if they are on the lowest level. So in some enterprises the entry title is sales manager followed by the title of sales director. This sometimes goes so far that even a sales VP is not even a cost centre manager. The reason behind this is that it helps the sales process if a manger is visited by a sales director; it will honour the manager and make him/her more likely to buy.

So if gathering requirements for the business architecture do not be fouled on tittles in the sales area.

5.3.6.1.1 Strategic planning

The sales business owner will usually start the strategic planning with his/her counterpart in marketing to arrive at a strategic plan that will detail the areas that sales will focus with priorities thereof. This process has a heavy dependency on the market research in the campaign to sale process but requires very little IS help apart from some reports.

5.3.6.1.2 Flexible modelling

Once a strategic plan has been formulate a modelling exercise based on previous data needs to be attempted. As discussed in the campaign to sale process this requires a very good analytical data warehouse that is capable of predictive modelling.

5.3.6.1.3 Rolling forecast

The Sales department will always need to provide the rest of the business with forecasts. For this a process a system will need to be established that will continuously gather the forecasts reports from all the sales teams and correlate them. The sales teams in most enterprises are consisting of an internal and an external sales force.

Sometimes the sales force themselves are not seeing the customers direct but selling through retailers or intermediaries. If that is the case the collaboration required for solid forecasts may need a different and more complex set-up and will need to be decided before starting on any solution architecture.

5.3.6.1.4 Collaborative planning

The collaborative processes are not limited to the forecast, but when but selling through retailers or intermediaries' collaboration also needs to happen across organisations. The collaboration in selling will of course also include the internal sales team.

5.3.6.1.5 Supply chain integration

If the sales process is based on products the sales efforts need to be integrated into the supply chain so that the sales team is aware of the availability of the sellable goods and how long the waiting list for none available goods will be so that the customers or intermediaries will be fully informed. A sales process that will not offer this feature will always be flawed as the sales person will have a hard time in front of the customer.

5.3.6.1.6 Planning cycle monitoring

Since the sales planning within some enterprises can get quite complex due to the complexity of the sales organisation and sheer mass of stakeholders it is a good idea to have a process that is helping with the monitoring of the plan. It should be stated however that this process makes only sense in one of four enterprises.

5.3.6.1.7 Performance reviews

Reviewing performance in sales is quite different to the yearly performance review in the hire-to-retire process. The performance review in sales is often done on a monthly or even shorter base with a constant push on higher performance or more sales, more profit or on another parameter such as the sales of a specific product; in sales it very normal that every month there will be special bonuses on a defined performance.

In some organisations where sales is paid on bonuses only the performance reviews will be more focused in helping the sales persons to realise potentials rather then to measure them. From an IT perspective a solid reporting as well a good training system is required.

5.3.6.1.8 Sales planning & forecasting guides

This process will focus on creating and distributing templates independent to the sales force to enable them to plan their activities better and help them in forecasting.

Sometimes it makes sense to provide them with offline tools not because there may be problem with internet connections, but mainly because the sales force will often not trust IT and their management of not "listening in" to their activities, so they will use Excel instead.

At this point it also important to explain a bit on the use and limitations of CRM systems; CRM systems are ideal for all sales, marketing and customer service activity that follows a strict a mature process that takes place within an office environment.

However it should not be implemented instead of process maturity as this will then just lead to the fact that everyone is trying to use some fields, while others use other fields for the same information.

When approaching a mobile sales force some CRM vendors will push for mobile clients or web enabled GUI. This however is not a good idea as the adoption rate of the integrated use of the tools range lower than 5 % in the mobile sales force. Most mobile sales people will just log in once a day a try to recollect all activities.

Good mobile sales people on the other hand are much more focused on the customer and the relationship with him rather than using IT tools for logging information; IT tools are only used for presenting.

As the most effective sales people, are person orientated there are many good processes where there is a shared service centre that will record the visits for the sales person phoning in with his/her impressions and then briefing the sales person on the next visit, the shared centre staff than will use the CRM system.. It should be noted that this process with a heavy manual component is only of use if the sales person is selling face to face.

5.3.6.1.9 Account planning

The process of account planning is an operational way to classify customers and prospective customers to ensure that the time invested is best used.

Most companies follow an A-D classification that is needed to be available in the sales or CRM systems.

Within the account planning process the parameters that govern the classification are constantly updated, as well the measurements checked against results. The classification is usually mainly focussed on the turn over and the expected units sold. The enterprise architect will need to ensure that this process is feed with the right business intelligence.

5.3.6.1.10 Opportunity planning

Apart from the main sales lines there are often opportunities that need to recorded and classified. The optimal outcome of this process from the point of the enterprise is the identification of a profitable cross selling opportunity that will increase sales and profits without any major changes or investments needed.

The best support for this process is in an self service suggestion system (sometimes with reward) and then consequently an investment planning tool that will allow for sales scenario modelling reuse of the existing sales support systems.

5.3.6.2 Sales performance management

Sales performance management is the most important process and mandatory week to week process for sales managers to report on sales realised and sales expected.

5.3.6.2.1 Pipeline performance management

The pipeline performance management process is about the reporting of the sales expected for the next sales period that every sales person will create. Pipeline reports consist of a list of all customers with the expected revenue, the probability and optionally some comments. The sales person will then also add the sales expected from prospective customers.

The information from each sales person will then be aggregated and often corrected by the managers to reflect the forecast abilities of their team members.

The resulting pipeline report will then be used by the operational executives to plan for delivery. The reports will then also be compared with the real figures at the end of the period and used to identify training or mentoring for the sales force.

5.3.6.2.2 Sales pipeline analytic

The sales pipeline report process then consists of the sales realised against the each customer divided into a few categories. The reason for the process is to identify customers that have ordered much less in the previous periods and to identify and counteract their actions towards gaining a larger share again. It is important to be able to flag customers going into administration or similar to be excluded from the reports.

318

5.3.6.2.3 Territory management

Most sales forces define a territory where a sales person will be responsible for as this is the best way to keep sales persons from poaching their good customers from each other. Sometimes there are also multiple sales organisations with different segments in a territory that need to be managed.

5.3.6.2.4 Market segmentation

The market segmentation is an ever moving process, so segments should NEVER be set up as anything close to static data. There are a number of systems that do this.

The market segmentation process needs to detail all the market segment ownership in terms of customers and of product and services, as well as describe an operational procedure on conflicts.

So it could happen that a pharmaceutical enterprise segments its sales force into a heart related drug segment and a segment for all other drugs. So in this example it will happen that the same doctor is visited by two sales representatives from the same company unless he only specialises on heart conditions. Some doctors will like this approach with more expertise, but others may reject it so that the operational procedure from the market segmentation will need to provide guidance on these conflicts.

5.3.6.2.5 Territory assignment & scheduling

The process is to split the overall map of a country into territories in an objective way and schedule the assignment of the territories in priorities

5.3.6.2.6 Territory / organizational mapping

This process is to assign a sales representative to a territory and map the assignments into the organisational chart as well as into all the CRM systems, so that if a customer or potential customer contacts the enterprise the sales representative will be informed automatically to ensure best customer service.

5.3.6.2.7 Rule-based synchronization for mobile devices

Some organisation will give their mobile sales force tools that can be used offline. So this process will decide what part of the data needs to be synchronised when so that the sales representative does not need to worry about this.

An example could be an order taken and the software on his PC will know that the due time for orders that need to reach the customer the next day is 16:30, the system will attempt to send the data even if the whole sales day is not finished.

5.3.6.2.8 Sales analysis by territory

It is quite important for the individual sales representative to have reports specific for his territory. They should also include data on a geographical basis as this will mean much more to the sales representative than pure addresses or customer names since most sales representative have a very good analytical mind on pictures while a pure text based report is less appealing to them.

5.3.6.2.9 Interface to third-party territory planning tools

Since there is the need for lots of geographical data in the territory planning process there is usually the need to interface some of the information with external sources

5.3.6.3 Accounts & contacts

This level 2 process is all about the day to day business of the account management itself by the individual sales representative.

5.3.6.3.1 Visit planning

This process is to schedule the appointments with customers or prospective customers. For this it is beneficial to use automatic scheduling software with GIS functionality that is customisable to include lunches and variants on visit times; only that way it is possible to use the time of each sales representative to the best possible means. Please note that the booking of visits is done via service centres, so they need to have access to the parameter entered by the sales representative as well.

5.3.6.3.2 Fact sheet

Fact sheet production is on of the sales assistance processes that are sometimes done by marketing that will work a fact sheet on frequently asked question to the individual sales representative. The fact sheets are usually a good utility to communicate the most important facts and are often used for basic presentation at the customer side.

5.3.6.3.3 Interaction history

Since most sales representatives will visit customers on regular basis such as every month the full details of the last visit may not be in the present memory, so that is why an interaction history is of importance. Sometimes it might be good to have the sales representative record these interactions verbally while he/she is driving to the next customer and have same then transcribed.

5.3.6.3.4 Activity management

Before starting the visit at a customer site or via phone it is important to refresh the memory on the most important activities that will need to be performed and note them down as a check list.

5.3.6.3.5 Email & fax integration

The communication integration process needs to enable the sales representative to communicate important information with each customer without a complicated search for emails or fax numbers.

5.3.6.3.6 Relationship management

For sales people it is important to record and retrieve information on the relationship of customers and their specific needs ("Mr. B your former teacher also bought this product yesterday")

5.3.6.3.7 Marketing attributes

The sales representative need to be enabled to set marketing attributes for each customers, such as include this company with a medium gift on the next special occasion or send the customer information on service B12 when it goes live.

5.3.6.3.8 Customer specific pricing

A very common feature is the variable pricing for each customer either on a blanket discount basis or on special prices for each item.

The goal of the enterprise is always to charge as much as possible without making the average customer go mad if he finds out that he could have spent less, which is called list price.

When implementing special prices most ERP systems will operate with specific discounts on the various products and determine the maximum range of a discount that can only be changed on special deals where the customer will buy another product on list price so that at the end of the order there is still a margin left.

Another part of the customer specific pricing is the waving of the postage & packing fees. So as an enterprise architect you will need to ensure that these minimum requirements are in place.

5.3.6.3.9 Account planning

From the previous processes the sales representative will have the information on how important each customer is and how the territory requires to be visited. Since each customer now will have special needs such as a preferred calling time for sales representatives this process will need to be fine tuned to the accounts activity to the degree that the sales management in the enterprise will allow. So this standard process needs to be highly customisable.

5.3.6.3.10 Customer analysis

There is also the need for reports specific for each customer, often on previous order, payment history and amounts outstanding as well as on a product or service breakdown structure ("if he buys lots of screws why is he not buying any nuts")

5.3.6.3.11 Account classification

As discussed previous the general classification of accounts is done via the sales executive, however there may be special circumstances in terms of accounts that are influential in an area that however have little turnover (e.g. lab equipment at an university) that need to be reclassified by the sales representative himself.

5.3.6.4 Opportunity management

If the definition of opportunity is down to most sales persons everything is an opportunity, so if you talk this process through make certain that opportunities capture all the special areas that are not covered by the regular processes.

5.3.6.4.1 Opportunity planning

The first process will be on planning the execution of opportunities mainly to ensure that the opportunities are spread through the year and to ensure that any additional resources are present. For this process some services from project management can be reused.

5.3.6.4.2 Team selling

Team selling is the process where many sales people will work together at a customer meeting. This is often used if there is specific knowledge on the part of some members of the team that will benefit the sales effort. Another well used example of the process is when one sales representative is very successful in selling a specific product or service to use him/her to assist their colleagues on a sales call so that the other sales person will benefit by learning his/her technique. This process requires very little in terms of IS

5.3.6.4.3 Competitive information

Competitive Information or Intelligence is a process to document the strength and weaknesses of the competition including their price structure and the details of their sales portfolio. The best source of the information is the sales force that has direct contact with the customers and will hear this information on a daily basis, whereas the sales and marketing management urgently require this information for their market research. The problem in this process is to capture the information in way that makes it possible to aggregate the information without severely limiting the input or to create too many mandatory fields.

5.3.6.4.4 Account specific sales processes

Some accounts such as very large enterprises or public organisations require a specific sales process such as purchasing only through Requests for Proposals (RFP). In these circumstances the sales or CRM system will need to be flexible enough to implement the specific sales process in a very fast time without special IT support.

5.3.6.4.5 Automatic business partner assignment

Once customers contact an enterprise the sales or CRM system will have to have a system to assign a specific sales representative. The process needs to take all the specifics such as segmentation and territory into account and when required ask the potential customer these questions.

5.3.6.4.6 Pricing

The pricing process for special opportunities needs to allow for strategic needs, bundling and therefore be separate from the normal pricing.

5.3.6.4.7 Activities

The activity management process on opportunities will also need to be separated and be able not to follow a prescribed route, as often opportunities are used to refine new approaches

5.3.6.4.8 Follow-up transactions

Within the opportunity management process there is the need to follow up transactions to allow for readjustments to the overall process.

5.3.6.4.9 Product configuration

The product configuration process enables the sales manger to create new and special products to explore opportunities. This is a common way to a special price in bundling existing products and is very often done in the fast moving consumer good and telecommunications (special rates for mobiles) areas. This process ideally requires a business rule engine for fast adoption.

5.3.6.4.10 Anticipated revenue

The anticipated revenue process in opportunity management is the trickiest process in the opportunity management process, as due to the nature of trying new concepts a solid forecast model is hardly possible, the sales mangers will have to analyse the market potential and build a forecast model themselves.

As this usually turns out not to be feasible the process is often replaced by a pure guess on behalf of the sales managers with the exception of the opportunity being created as one of bidding, in which case the revenue will be calculated with the help of some project mangers that will have to analyse the complete bid and to perform a cost analysis.

5.3.6.4.11 Buying centre

Some opportunities are created to sell some products and services into a complex organisation. At that point the buying centre process will describe the roles, influence and decision powers of all the persons involved. The buying centre process will then to ensure that the right customer representatives are approached in all stages.

5.3.6.4.12 Sales project management

As some opportunities such as bids or bundling of very high priced items and services reach such a high complexity that a pure product configuration will not do a sales project management process is required to construct this complex product or service. The process needs to be guided with a system that is a hybrid of a product configuration management tool and a project system. However since these kinds of tools are often not available in the time that the sales opportunity exist, the process often results with a huge amount of manual effort. The enterprise architect with the CIO should at least try to sort out this problem beforehand to reduce the costs of opportunity management.

5.3.6.4.13 Opportunity hierarchies

The opportunity hierarchy process will break complex opportunities into smaller easier to mange opportunities with the sales system in place to record the dependencies.

5.3.6.4.14 Sales process & selling methodologies

This process is in place to the sales process by providing the right templates and process information at every stage of the sales process, as well as to alert sales management if certain predefined selling processes and methodologies are not applied

5.3.6.4.15 Opportunity analysis

The opportunity analysis will monitor expected revenues, the opportunity pipeline, progress towards opportunity completion and opportunity success. The process feeds the information back into the sales cycle by using the results to discover which customers to target in subsequent marketing campaigns.

5.3.6.5 Quotation & order management

Selling is done in two ways. The first is selling with a fixed price such as often done with pharmaceutical products or in general retailing, while the second way is to negotiate the price and conditions. The quotation and order management process is more aimed on the second way and less so in the first way. When dealing with fixed prices it is mainly the order management that will be used. Any negotiations when your customer is a whole-seller such as volume discounts or special discounts are part of the pricing & contract process, which is the next level 2 process and will not be done in this process.

5.3.6.5.1 Quotations

Quotations are used only for goods or services that are not required instantly as the quote will first need to be processed. The quotation process will always start with a request that needs to contain the requesters name and contact, the description of the requested service and/or product, the quantity, the required return of the quote and the required date of delivery.

The system will then need to first check if the service and/or product can be delivered at all and if it is necessary to involve a manual check (often needed for complex services). If the system will not detect a manual override the system will first search for the conditions that were entered for the customer or prompt for the information. Then it will calculate the quote and release it to the representative, who will then deicide if it is valid and send it to the customer.

The quote will be stored. If the quote requires a manual quote it will be routed to the internal quotation officer via a work flow who will then manually create the offer, pre-check on availability, send it via a workflow for approval (the work flow chosen usually depends on the size of the quote) and then send it to the customer as well as to log it.

5.3.6.5.2 Package quotation

When quotes are required for more complex inquiries such as a combination of products and services a very similar process as before will happen with the main difference that the process will contain an element of strategic pricing that will reduce the price of one quote component to allow generating a the revenue with another component.

A very basic example of this is to purchase a software license with a discount of 95 %, but that includes maintenance for 5 years as well. So the profit in this case will be made with the maintenance fees. This kind of packaged quotation is often used as most businesses only look at the first off costs and not on the 5 year TCO.

5.3.6.5.3 Order capture

Order capture on complex projects is quite straight forward as it only relates back to the quotation and will usually be followed by contract negotiations. However orders with a very high number of order lines or a high number of orders such as in an online retailer requires an automatic process.

After any received order it is important that an order acknowledgment is sent back to the customer informing him/her on the order number and the next steps. Some orders such in retail will also contain billing information, while this is less common in other areas.

The final part of the order capture is then to initiate the delivery and billing processes.

5.3.6.5.4 Automatic business partner assignment

This process will ensure that all the involved business partners are informed of the order. In many scenarios this will then create an order on their side. An example would be to place an order with a large online retailer and the retailer then ordering a business partner to deliver the goods.

5.3.6.5.5 Order status tracking

A very important process is the order status tracking that needs to be displayable both in the order systems as well as on a secure customer portal. The order status tracking will need to be closely integrated in the order fulfilment system that is initiating all the steps that are required for the order process.

5.3.6.5.6 Pricing

Some orders will take their price from the quotation, while others will use the price multiplied with the discount factor. It is important to remember that the pricing is not only determine by the services and/or products, but will also include extra costs such packaging or travel costs for service providers. This is also where the real tricky part of integration into 3rd party systems comes into effect.

5.3.6.5.7 Price change approval

Prices are fluctuating, however if prices change a process needs to ensure that the price change is implemented in a way according to the terms with the customers (often needs written 30 days notice) and is approved by all the stakeholders in the enterprise.

5.3.6.5.8 Order validation check

If an order arrives at the enterprise it may not be deliverable at all or not at the desired time. The process will first need to check for availability for the order at the given time. If the ordered services and/or products are available at the requested time the overall delivery process will continue.

If the order can be delivered, but not in time or only partially, the customer needs to be informed and unless she/he cancels the order usually the available items will be delivered and the ones that are not available will need to put on back order.

The system will then look at all the back orders every day to decide when they can be processed. By splitting an order some companies will create a new order for the back ordered services and/or products and link it to the old one, others will keep the order open as not delivered.

The main difference on these finer points are usually in the fact that many companies can only bill on a full delivery or shipment in some legislation. Any order that cannot be delivered at all needs to be cancelled and the customer informed. Sometimes it is also important to inform the customer via the sales representative as the sales person may arrange for an alternative.

5.3.6.5.9 Credit management & credit check

If the customer has an account with your enterprise then the next step in the order processing is the credit management process. In this process there are a few factors that first need to be configured against a rule-set sin te first instance so that afterwards the process can be automated.

The most common once area about a customer credit rating is (usually supplied via interface integration by a credit rating agency) the payment history with the enterprise, the credit limit, any arrears and the amount of any outstanding balance.

In some cases your accounts may come up with some additional data required. If the credit management is not successful the customer needs to be contacted and upfront payment or cash on delivery (COD) option need to be suggested. Only if these options fail the order will be put on back order or cancelled with an interface to the sales bonus system.

5.3.6.5.10 Payment card processing

With most retail and some business customers a card payment is the first choice. For this it is important to get the full card details including security number(s), the postal address and the name of the card holder. The information will then be interfaced with the merchant bank that your company uses and either verified or not. If the payment cannot be verified another card needs to be taken into considerations. Alternative forms of payment in this process can also be an upfront payment or cash on delivery (COD).

5.3.6.5.11 Automated follow-up processes

Within the processing of some orders some other processes such as the global trade process for border crossings need to be initiated. Again here it is advisable to support this process with an easy configurable business rule engine.

5.3.6.5.12 Product authorisation & restriction

If your enterprise is selling restricted services and/or products such as weapons, uranium or morphine a product authorisation process will need to be triggered that almost always requires interfacing with public bodies. Once an authorisation has been granted the authorisation will be copied and supplied to all the forms used in the transaction as attachment with reference to the issuing authority.

5.3.6.5.13 Product configuration

If the order contains a product that needs to be manufactured this process will specify the product configuration.

5.3.6.5.14 Bill of Material

After a product is chosen to be manufactured this process will ensure that the right bill of materials (BOM) is ordered a booked against the order See S2P process for details.

If the services and/or products require no integration into the S2P process a BOM will be created for picking the order.

5.3.6.5.15 Availability check

If services and/or products are not covered by the "Product Configuration" process a second detailed availability check is performed following the same pattern the "Order Validation Check" process, but now also creating a delivery order to be processed and sent to the warehouse.

5.3.6.5.16 Rebates

Before starting the billing process a process to check on the availability of rebates such as if the invoice is paid in 10 days there will be a rebate on 2 % and add this into the billing process. Rebates are different from discounts as they require an outstanding action from the customer.

5.3.6.5.17 Billing

Billing should ideally be done just at the same time as the fulfilment of the order. The process will ensure that the bill contains all details as well as the order request reference from the customer and will explain any discounts and possible rebates.

Once the billing is completed the bill will be transferred to the account payable / collection process.

5.3.6.5.18 Fulfilment synchronisation

If all other steps are done this process will ensure that the shipment and the order will leave or ideally arrive at the customer at the same time

5.3.6.5.19 Quotation and order analysis

Since the quotation and order process are operational processes the analytics mainly requires reports on the overall process performance against the KPI's, the number of successful orders, the amount of orders per segment, the sales bonus payment on orders, the amount of quotation that were translated into order over the different time-lines, the average time from quote to order, the percentage of dormant quotes and many more. So it is important to capture this list by asking yourself on every process what could be required as the stakeholders are most likely on to see the reports as the outcome of implementing the system.

5.3.6.6 Pricing & contract

The second way of the order process is towards customised contracts that are collaborated with the customer rather than using a predefined set of services and/or products. In this process services and/or products are released by request rather than ordered.

5.3.6.6.1 Value & quantity contracts

A very common type of sales contract for services and/or products is the value & quantity contracts, where the customer signs up for a value or quantity to be delivered when he is asking for it. Examples are suppliers in the automotive industry or IT consultancy services.

These contracts are set very similar to pre paid accounts, just that the billing is usually still done on a monthly basis unless the customer does not use the contract up, in which case the rest will just be billed (which never really happens).

5.3.6.6.2 Sales agreements

Sales agreements are the second type of common sales contracts. They define the framework under which the services and/or products are released.

5.3.6.6.3 Authorized customers

All sales contracts may only be executed by customers or persons at the customers that have the authorisation to do so, as these contracts can easily be misappropriated. So the system will need to ensure that the authorisation is genuine.

5.3.6.6.4 Contract completion rules

Contracts have very special rules that govern when a task that is defined as a fixed price contract can be seen as complete. If this process is not performed very tight it often ends in courts with huge repercussions.

5.3.6.6.5 Collaborative contract negotiation

A third less common approach that will also be discussed in the source to pay process is that of collaborate contracts. These contracts see both the selling enterprise and the customer as business partners rather then as seller and buyer. Usually the seller instead of receiving money for his services and/or products will be linked into the revenue and will share the risk with the buyer. This kind of contract is common in the production of very expensive and research intensive industries such as the production and research of aeroplanes. On the negotiation process both parties will have to agree in detail on their responsibilities. The result then need to be configured into the ERP systems which is a very time consuming task that however need to be done very conscientious as both parties share a high financial risk. In this area it is also important that both ERP systems are synchronised.

5.3.6.6.6 Release order processing

When receiving an order from the customer the contract process is queried if the services and/or products can be released. There is usually no further work done.

5.3.6.6.7 Cancellation handling

Cancellation are a bit of a tricky subject in the sales contracts as they often carry fines, so a cancellation needs to be handled very different on the contract side.

5.3.6.6.8 Fulfilment synchronisation

The fulfilment synchronisation in the contract sales area is mainly seen as the shipment information interfaced to the supply chain of the customer.

5.3.6.6.9 Automatic business partner assignment

This process will ensure that all the involved business partners are informed of the order. In many scenarios this will then create an order on their side.

5.3.6.6.10 Product configuration

If the order contains a product that needs to be manufactured this process will specify the product configuration. This process is the same as in the previous level 2 process.

5.3.6.6.11 Contract status tracking

The contract status tracking in contracts is mainly used by the customer as an automatic feed into his supply chain process.

5.3.6.6.12 Credit management & credit check

In some special circumstances such as known problems with a customer a similar process to the credit management & credit check in "Quotation & Order Management" will take place.

5.3.6.6.13 Pricing

All pricing is done either customer specific or it follows the list prices for contracts. The non regulated pricing are often expenses occurred during the performance of services.

5.3.6.6.14 Customer specific pricing

The pricing on contracts is done as an amendment or a schedule to the contract and then entered into the system. The amendment or schedule is normally changed or updated in regular period or if the contract is extended by new services and/or products.

5.3.6.6.15 Promotional pricing

Occasional there will be a promotional pricing done in contracts mainly to push the customer in new services and/or products. The system will then have to use these prices unless they are higher than the customer specific prices (which also happen occasional).

5.3.6.6.16 Contract analysis

Finally the contract analysis in sales will be used mainly to identify areas of improvement, incident & problem reports and to find additional sales opportunities

5.4 Value check

Implementing standard business processes will save on costs as the business & solution architecture can be reused as well using some industry standard software.

Risks are avoided by using proven processes instead of creating new ones and starting to do all the errors and issues again that were performed by others beforehand.

The time to market will also improve significantly as the solutions on process and system side can be copied from other experiences (reuse).

However a certain problem occurs with measuring the ROI, reduced risk and better time to market as this will only work if there is honest reference data of the situation before. This can turn a bit tricky on areas such as risk, because in a chaotic setting the risk might not even have been identified beforehand.

Appendix

A. Complete IS Processes

Strategy

+ **Market Definition**

* Competitive Services & strategy

* Understand Customers

* Identify Opportunities

* Classify Opportunities

+ **Define strategic Assets**

* Define Services

* Define Priorities

* Define risk & compliance profile

+ Develop Offerings with financials

* Describe Market Space

* Define high level service offerings on a need basis

* Budget offerings

* Create Service Portfolios

+ Execute strategy

* Create strategic alignment plans

* Set Objectives

* Align strategic assets with customers

* Define Critical Success Factors (CSF)

* Explore Business Potentials

* Conduct Competitive Analysis and readjust

* Define KPI's and set Business expectations

* Segment Service Offerings into Service Portfolios

* Communicate strategy

Portfolio/Programme Management

+ **Define Programmes**

* Define change required

* Create Vision for better future and communicate

* Create benefit & threat matrix

* Define value add

* Design a coherent delivery capability

* Learn from experience and readjust

* Ensure alignment with strategy

+ **Establish Programmes**

* Define Business Case

* Establish Risk matrix

* Develop quality standards

* Create Delivery Organisation & Budgets

* Establish leadership and stakeholder management

* Create benefit realisation plan

* Create Blueprints and delivery plan

* Establish control and planning framework

+ **Close Programmes**

* Monitor progress

* Check for realisation of capabilities

* Control Benefits

* Close programme

Project Management

+ Starting

* Appoint PM and sponsor

* Prepare Project Brief

* Define project board

* Create project approach

* Appoint project board

+ Initiation

* Define Quality standards

* Create a high level project plan

* Refine the Business Case and Risk matrix

* Set up project controls

* Set up a project library

* Assemble wider team

* Create Project Initiation team

+ **Planning**

* Design a plan for the project plan

* Define all Services in detail

* Identify activities & dependencies

* Estimation

* Scheduling

* Analyse Risks

* Complete Plan

+ **Directing**

* Create plan for management approval

* Communicate plan & readjust (danger of macro & micro-management)

* Authorise activities

* Prepare for Stage and exception points

* Programme board approval on Stages and exceptions

* Giving ad hoc direction

* Manage project change process

+ **Managing project delivery**

* Create work packages

* Assign work packages

* Control delivery of work packages

* Control budget

* Control risk & compliance management

+ **Managing Stage Boundaries**

* Planning Stages

* Updating project plan

* Updating project and business case

* Report on stage progress

* Manage Exception plan

+ **Control stages**

* Assess progress of project against plan

* Adjust Plan

* Capture project issues

* Manage project issues

* Report to stakeholders highlights on progress and issues

* Escalate project issues

+ **Closing**

* Decommission of project

* Identify Follow up Actions

* Delegate Follow up Actions

* Evaluate Project

Design/Architecture

+ Business Architecture

* Define Business Objectives

* Develop Priorities (Financial, Legal and Competitive)

* Identify enterprise business process assets

* Decide on new standard Business Architecture Assets to implement

* Design non standard Business Processes

* Develop Business Services

+ SLM (create)

* Understand Financial, Legal and Competitive factors

* Understand KPI for higher management

* Draw SLA drafts (inc. Security, Capacity, Availability, Continuity, Service Operation (Incident, Problem, Alert, etc.) and Risk Management)

* Discuss and agree SLA

* Budget for SLR's in Business Services

354

* Create Plan for SLM (for transition with explanations)

+ **Data and Solution Architecture**

* Translate Business Services into Technical Services as Solution Architecture (Supplier)

* Create Data requirements

* Identify data reuse and additional data requirements

* Develop Data Architecture

* Create Solution Architecture on Work Packages

* Integrate SLM into Solution Architectures

* Create Designs

* Create Test plans and test scripts

* Identify Opportunities

* Design Migrations

* Conduct Governance

+ **Technology Architecture**

* Identify all technical Services required

* Create overall technical architecture

* Create Technical Architecture on Work Packages

* Integrate SLM into Technical Architectures

* Create Designs

* Create Test plans and test scripts

* Identify Opportunities

* Design Migrations

* Conduct Governance

+ **Execution**

* Create development environments

* Develop solution

* Deploy Solution

* Create test environments

* Create live environments

* Conduct Dress Rehearsals

356

+ **Test**

* Conduct Unit Tests

* Conduct Integration Tests

* Conduct Systems Tests

* Conduct User Acceptance Tests

* Conduct SLM Tests

Transition

+ Asset & Configuration Management

* Planning & Identification

* Control of Services Catalogues with SLM

* Status Reporting

* License Management

+ Change Management

* Registration

* Configuration

* Assessment

* Authorisation

* Plan & Control

* Scheduling Changes

* Measurement & Reporting

* Emergency Change

+ **Release & Deployment Management**

* Planning

* Build & Test Cycle

* Deployment

* Retirement

* Early Life Support

* Release Review

Operations

+ Request Management

* Detecting and Logging

* Categorise

* Prioritise

* Investigate

* Resolution

* Closure

* Review

+ Incident Management

* Identification & logging

* Categorise

* Initial Investigation

* Escalate

* Prioritise

* Investigate

* Resolution

* Closure

* Review

+ **Problem Management**

* Detecting and Logging

* Categorise

* Prioritise

* Investigate

* Resolution

* Closure

* Review

Alert or Event Management

* Service Monitoring

* Detecting and Logging

* Categorise

* Prioritise

* Investigate

* Resolution

* Closure

* Review

+ **SLM (ongoing)**

* Application Management

* Ongoing Reporting

* Technical Management

* Replacement management

* Customer Satisfaction Survey

+ **Access Management**

* Request Logging

* Request Verification

* Provide Access Rights

* Restrict/Remove Access Rights

* Maintain Roles & Groups

B. Standard Business Processes

Hire-to-Retire

Recruitment and Selection

- Sourcing Resumes

- Screening

- Offer closure

- New hire integration

- Compliance

- Self Service

Training and Development

- Needs analysis

- Administration

- Material creation

Benefits Administration

- Health & welfare (incl. Annual Enrollment, Research, Processing)

- Defined Benefits

- Defined Contributions

- Finance Administration

- ESS/MSS

Compensation Management

- Payroll

- Compensation review

- Stock and benefit in kind

- Bonus plan administration

- ESS/MSS

Performance Management

- Performance Review

- Progression management

- 360 Feedback

- ESS/MSS

Workforce Management

- Employee master data management

- Leave management

- Visa processing

- Time and attendance

- ESS/MSS

Separation Management

- Data management

- Clearance

- Exit interview

Customer contact to resolution

Service Order Management

- Service Order

- Quotation Service

- Order Processes

- Service Employee Resource Planning

- Service Confirmation Processing

- Product Service Letter Processing

- Logistics Integration Processes

- Service Order Analytic

Service Contract Management

- Service Agreement

- Service Contract Quotation Processing

- Service Contract Processing

- Usage Based Contract Management

- Service Level Management

- Value and Quantity Contracts

- Contract Determination

- Service Plan Processing

- Service Contract Analytic

Complaints & Returns

- Knowledge Management

- Complaints Processing

- Returns Processing

- Follow-Up Processes

- Recall Management

- Warehouse Management Integration

- Logistics Integration

- Financial Integration

- Complaints and Returns Analytic

Case Management

- Case Processing

- Change Request Management

- Service Confirmation Processing

- Activity Processing

- Supporting Processes

- Case Management Analytic

Warranty Management

- Customer and Vendor Warranty

- Product and Warranty Registration

- Warranty Determination

- Warranty Claim Processing

- Warranty Analysis

Plan to Produce

Production Planning

- Production Planning
- Capacity Planning
- Financial Integration

Manufacturing Execution

- Manufacturing Execution
- Shop Floor Integration
- Supervision and Control

Product Development

- Product Development
- Development Collaboration

Life-Cycle Data Management
370

- Document Management

- Product Structure Management

- Recipe Management

- Specification Management

- Change and Configuration Management

Campaign to sale

Marketing Resource Management

- Market Research

- Budget Planning

- Scenario Planning

- Marketing Planning and Budgeting

- Budget Control

- Product and Brand Planning

- Cost and Volume Planning

- Marketing Plan Analysis

- Marketing Calendar

- Marketing Organization

- Work flow and Approval

Segmentation & List Management

- Multiple Data Source Access

- High Speed Data Search

- Pre-Filtered/Personalized Attribute Lists

- Sampling and Splitting

- Embedded Predictive Modeling

- Personalized Filters

- Quick Counts

- Segment De duplication

- Suppression Filters

- Target Group Optimization

- Clustering

- Data Mining

- Decision Trees

- ABC Analysis

- List Management - List Format Mapping

- Duplicate Checks

- Postal Validation

- Data Cleansing

- Data Enrichment

- List Quality

- Lead and Activity Imports

- List Analysis

Campaign Management

- Campaign Planning

- Graphical Campaign Modelling

- Campaign Optimization

- Campaign Simulation

- Marketing Calendar

- Campaign-Specific Pricing

- Multichannel Campaign Execution

- Multi-wave Campaign Execution

- Event-Triggered Campaign Execution

- Real-Time Response Tracking

- Cost/Financial Reporting

- Personalized (e)Mails

- Bounce Handling

- Call Lists

- Campaign ROI

- Interactive Scripting

- Target Group Analysis

- Campaign Analysis

Lead Management

- Multiple Interaction Channels

- Automated Qualification

- Rule-Based Distribution

- Lead Dispatching

- Web-Based Lead Generation

- Lead Partner Management

- Mass Generation

- Response Recording

- Lead Surveys

- Automatic Generation of Follow-Up Activities

- Lead Analysis

Sales

Sales Planning & Forecasting

- Strategic Planning

- Flexible Modeling

- Rolling Forecast

- Collaborative Planning

- Supply Chain Integration

- Planning-Cycle Monitoring

- Performance Reviews

- Sales Planning & Forecasting Guides

- Account Planning

- Opportunity Planning

Sales Performance Management

- Pipeline Performance Management

- Sales Pipeline Analytic

Territory Management

- Market Segmentation

- Territory Assignment & Scheduling

- Territory/Organizational Mapping

- Rule-Based Synchronization for Mobile Devices

- Sales Analysis by Territory

- Interface to Third-Party Territory Planning Tools

Accounts & Contacts

- Visit Planning

- Fact Sheet

- Interaction History

- Activity Management

- Email & Fax Integration

- Relationship Management

- Marketing Attributes

- Customer specific Pricing

- Account Planning

- Customer Analysis

- Account Classification

Opportunity Management

- Opportunity Planning

- Team Selling

- Competitive Information

- Account specific Sales Processes

- Automatic Business Partner Assignment

- Pricing

- Activities

- Follow-Up Transactions

- Product Configuration

- Anticipated Revenue

- Buying Centre

- Sales Project Management

- Opportunity Hierarchies

- Sales Process & Selling Methodologies

378

- Opportunity Analysis

Quotation & Order Management

- Quotations

- Package Quotation

- Order Capture

- Automatic Business Partner Assignment

- Order Status Tracking

- Pricing

- Price Change Approval

- Order Validation Check

- Credit Management & Credit Check

- Payment Card Processing

- Automated Follow-Up Processes

- Product Authorization & Restriction

- Product Configuration

- Bill of Material

- Availability Check

- Rebates

- Billing

- Fulfilment Synchronisation

- Quotation and Order Analysis

Pricing & Contract (Order)

- Value & Quantity Contracts

- Sales Agreements

- Authorized Customers

- Contract Completion Rules

- Collaborative Contract Negotiation

- Release Order Processing

- Cancellation Handling

- Fulfillment Synchronization

- Automatic Business Partner Assignment

- Product Configuration

- Contract Status Tracking

- Credit Management & Credit Check

- Pricing

- Customer specific Pricing

- Promotional Pricing

- Contract Analysis

Record-to-Report (R2R)

General Accounting

- (AP,AR, GL, Accruals , Chart of accounts, GAAP, IFRS, etc.)

- Manual Journal Entries

- Automated Journal Entries

- Bank Statement Processing

- Bank Account Reconciliation's

- Payroll Posting & Reconciliation

- Inter-company Postings

- Accounts for Loans/ Investments

Income Statement

- Invoice Recording
- Expense Adjustments

Balance Sheet

- Fixed Assets vs. current & others
- Capitalization
- Depreciation
- Liabilities
- Intangible Assets, Equity

Cost Accounting

- ABC Implementation
- ABC Model Validation
- ABC Model Population & Maintenance

- PA Reporting

- PA Reconciliation

Financial Planning & Analysis

- Management Reporting

- Budgeting & Forecasting

- Taxation

- Internal Audit

- Treasury

- Business Unit Support

- Decision Support & Analysis

Closing

- Daily Interface Monitoring & Reconciliation

- Month-end Sub Ledger Close

- Month-end Foreign Exchange Revaluation

- Month-end General Ledger Close

- Balance Sheet Accounts Reconciliation

- Inter-company Reconciliation's

- Allocations

- Consolidation

- Population of Reporting Database

- Audit Support

Source To Pay (Procure to Pay)

Sourcing

- Market/Demand Analysis

- Develop Category Strategy

- Evaluate, Negotiate and Award

- Supplier Performance Management

- Contract Compliance and Savings Validation

- Supplier Adoption

- Catalogue Management and Content Management

- Contract Management

- Tactical/Low Value Buying and Fulfillment

Invoice Payment

- Assigning payment forms

- Scheduling payment runs

- Discount Realization

- Dynamic Discount Management

Invoice Receipt & Entry

- Invoice Receipt and Scanning

- EDI invoices

- Invoice Verification and Entry

Vendor Management

- Vendor Master Updates

- Vendor Help desk

- Supplier Portal

- Vendor Statement Reconciliation

- P-Card/Corporate Card Administration

- Expense Reports Processing

- Expense Reports Audit

Invoice Processing

- GL Coding

- Approval Management & matching

- Resolving Match Exceptions

- Discrepancy Resolution

- Price Difference Reconciliation

Analytic & Miscellaneous

- MIS Reporting

- Spend Analytic

- Inter-company reconciliation's

- VAT Reclaim

- Month-end AP-GL Reconciliation's

Supplier Management

Purchasing Governance

- Global Spend Analysis

- Category Management

- Compliance Management

Sourcing

- Central Sourcing Hub

- RFx / Auctioning

- Bid Evaluation & Awarding

Contract Management

- Legal Contract Repository

- Contract Authoring

- Contract Negotiation

- Contract Execution

- Contract Monitoring

Collaborative Procurement

- Self-Service Procurement Services

- Direct / Plan-Driven Procurement

- Catalogue Content Management

Supplier Collaboration

- Web-based Supplier Interaction

- Direct Document Exchange

- Supplier Network

Supply Base Management

- Supplier Identification & On boarding

- Supplier Development & Performance Management

- Supplier Portfolio Management

Data Exchange & Legal Requirements

- Traceability and Environmental Compliance

- Global Data Synchronization

Time-to-Market

- New Product Development and Introduction

- Life-cycle Data Management

Quote To Cash or Order to Cash

Quotes & Proposals

- Lead Management

- Quoting

- Pricing

- Catalogue Management

Order Operations

- Order Entry and Scheduling

- Order Validation

- Credit Review and Management

- Order Booking

- On-hold Order Release

- Order Change/Expedite/Cancellations

- Contract Management

Shipment

- Article list production

- Packaging Management

- Freight Management

- Planning & Dispatching

- Allocation of articles

- Picking list creation

- Execution of picking list

- Packaging

- Freight Allocation

Customer Invoicing/Billing

- Collection of Billing Information

- Invoice Consolidation

- Invoice Presenting

- Revenue Assurance

Accounts Receivable/Collections Management

- Cash Application

- Collections

- Dispute Management

- Deductions Processing

- Credit Note Processing

- Account Reconciliation

- Cash Flow Forecasting

Financial Planning & Analysis (FP&A)

Budgeting/Forecasting

- Preparation of Budgets (different budgets, consolidation)

- Creation of Standard Models / Templates (user focus)

- Trend Analysis (analytics, difference in DWH)

- Historical Data Analysis (data migration, clean data)

- Budgeted vs Forecast (remember change, clear division, logs,..)

- Tracking the actual against the budget (excel vs. application -> version)

- Assumptions validation (difficult in electronic systems)

Reporting Overall

- Sales Reporting (performance, people)

- Cost Reporting (PA, ABC)

- Segment Reporting

- Competitor Analysis (data in?)

Internal Audit

- Internal Control Assessment

- Auditing of Financial Controls, Operational and Statutory Controls

- Review of Corporate Governance Structure

- Periodic Assessments

- Internal Checks

Taxation

- Transfer Pricing Reporting (pricing of contributions (assets, tangible and intangible, Services, and funds) transferred within an organization)

- Tax Calculations and Analysis

- Tax Filings

- Tax Accounting (cash, accrual, and other methods)

- Tax Planning

- VAT Support

- Foreign Tax Credit   reduce or eliminate double taxation

- Preparation of Tax Schedules

Treasury

- Advisory Services on currency exposure

- Disclosure requirements

- Monitoring equity, investments and income a/c

- Inter company a/c reconciliation

- Cash Management

- Restructuring funding structures

Cooperate Services

Corporate Affairs

- Statutory Reporting

- Competitive Intelligence

- Strategic Planning

- Corporate Tax Returns

- Industry Data Submission

- Rating Agencies Support

Real Estate Management

- Portfolio Management

- Commercial Real Estate Management

- Corporate Real Estate Management

- Facilities Management

- Support Processes

Enterprise Asset Management

- Investment Planning & Design

- Procurement & Construction

- Maintenance & Operations

- Decommission & Disposal

- Asset Analytic & Performance Optimization

- Takeover/Handover for technical objects

Project and Portfolio Management

- Project Planning

- Resource and Time Management

- Project Execution

- Project Accounting

- Prototyping and Ramp-Up

- Development Collaboration

Travel Management

- Travel Request and Pre-trip approval

- Travel Planning - Online Booking

- Travel and Expense Management

- Global Travel Policy Compliance

- Travel and Expense Analytic

Environment, Health, and Safety Compliance Management

- Environment, Health & Safety (EH&S)

- Environmental Compliance

- Recycling Administration

- Compliance for Products

Quality Management

- Quality Engineering

- Quality Assurance / Control

- Quality Improvement

- Audit Management

Global Trade

Export Management

- Export Classification

- Export Compliance

- Outbound Customs Services

- Outbound Trade Finance Services

- Electronic Compliance Reporting

Import Management

- Import Classification

- Import Compliance

- Inbound Customs Services

- Inbound Trade Finance Services

- Electronic Compliance Reporting

Trade Preference Management

- Vendor Declaration Handling

- Preference Calculation

- Customer Declaration Handling

Restitution Management

- Securities and Licenses Handling

- Restitution Contract Handling

- Recall Restitution Handling

- Restitution Calculation

Supply Chain

Demand & Supply Planning

- Demand Planning & Forecasting

- Safety Stock Planning

- Supply Network Planning

- Distribution Planning

- Service Parts Planning

Procurement

- Strategic Sourcing

- Purchase Order Processing

- Invoicing

Manufacturing

- Production Planning & Detailed Scheduling

- Manufacturing Visibility & Execution & Collaboration

- MRP based Detailed Scheduling

Warehousing

- Inbound Processing & Receipt Confirmation

- Outbound Processing

- Cross Docking

- Warehousing & Storage

- Physical Inventory

Order Fulfilment

- Sales Order Processing

- Billing

- Service Parts Order Fulfillment

Transportation

- Freight Management

- Planning & Dispatching

- Rating & Billing & Settlement

- Driver & Asset Management

- Network Collaboration

Real World Awareness

- Supply Chain Event Management

- Auto ID / RFID and Sensor Integration

Supply Chain Visibility

- Supply Chain Design

- Supply Chain Analytic

- Supply Chain Risk Management

- Sales & Operations Planning

Supply Network Collaboration

- Supplier Collaboration

- Customer Collaboration

- Outsourced Manufacturing

ABOUT THE AUTHOR

Cay Hasselmann is an experienced architect who has an exceptional track record in delivering cost savings and improving quality at the same time. He demonstrated this on numerous occasions and is happy to supply this.

He is also know for his track record on upward and downward communication, management, leadership and his ability to effectively communicate complex technical subjects in an easy and convincing manner and as such also direct the investment into the most business critical areas and reduce the overall IT spend.

Cay has extensive work experience in integrating ERP systems such as SAP and with integration (ESB, SOA,...), with which he has worked over 20 years. He also possesses a solid overall experience with virtually all technologies in all areas of architecture. He also is an industry leader in Service Strategy and Service Design and has implemented many ITIL implementations and integrated them into architectural frameworks such as TOGAF and Zachman.

He is a trusted adviser on all levels and has an exceptional talent for transferring his knowledge and techniques.

Cay Hasselmann is also the host of the leading (most subscribers) Enterprise Architecture pod cast "Critical Enterprise Architecture" found at http://cea.podbean.com/

www.ingramcontent.com/pod-product-compliance
Lightning Source LLC
Chambersburg PA
CBHW080144060326
40689CB00018B/3840